Life Talk for a Daughter

Life Talk for a Daughter

Emotional wisdom and practical survival skills
on 60 of life's most significant issues

Izabella Little

SPRING HILL

Published by Spring Hill

Spring Hill is an imprint of
How To Books Ltd
Spring Hill House
Spring Hill Road
Begbroke
Oxford
OX5 1RX
Tel: 01865 375794
info@howtobooks.co.uk
www.howtobooks.co.uk

British Library Cataloguing in Publication Data
A catalogue record of this book is available from the British Library

ISBN: 978-1-905862-06-1

Cover Design by Mousemat Design Ltd
Produced for How To Books by Deer Park Productions, Tavistock
Designed and typeset by Mousemat Design Ltd
Printed and bound by Bell & Bain Ltd, Glasgow

NOTE: The material contained in this book is set out in good faith for general guidance and
no liability can be accepted for loss or expense incurred as a result of relying in particular
circumstances on statements made in the book. Laws and regulations are complex and liable
to change, and readers should check the current position with relevant authorities before
making personal arrangements.

Contents

Part three: Practical stuff

Part four: Challenges and problems

In Conclusion

Izabella Little's parents were Polish and she was born in Kenya. She grew up in the Kenyan and Tanzanian bush, was the only girl at a boy's school for a number of years and completed her schooling in South Africa.

Izabella went on to study and work in the field of Information Technology (IT), headed up the IT department for a civil engineering company and started a company in 1985, specialising in IT Contracting and Human Resource solutions. It (SilverLine) grew fast and soon became a market leader.

She led the South African industry's representations to government concerning the Labour Relations Act and its implications for the IT Contracting industry and headed up a region of the Computing Services Association. Izabella spoke at a number of conferences and wrote articles for the IT media on a regular basis. In 1988 she had her beloved daughter (the original inspiration for *Life Talk for a Daughter*).

SilverLine was sold to Dimension Data, a leading South African IT group, in 1998 and a couple of years later Izabella encountered health problems which forced her to give up her business career.

She then started studying photography (her passion and hobby) and wrote *Life Talk For a Daughter*. Since the book's launch in South Africa Izabella's time is filled with handling readers' enthusiastic responses, giving talks on related subjects, learning about flower farming, spending as much time as possible in the wilderness, writing the much demanded *Life Talk for Sons*, and being Mum to her teenage daughter.

Izabella's 'mission' now is to work with the youth and to give them as much food for thought as possible concerning their life's direction, challenges and decisions. The contents of this book covers a number of situations which many of us will inevitably encounter along our life's journey, and Izabella provides a tool-kit of useful tips, hints and guidelines which make the journey that little bit smoother.

This book is dedicated
to
my daughter Dominique –
my inspiration and the light of my life.

introduction

This book began at the time my daughter was five years old. I realised that I wouldn't always be around and yet I had so many thoughts and feelings I wanted to share. I started writing letters to her about the topics that were close to my heart, for all those times when a daughter may wonder what her mother would have said about something.

Much of what I have written about is what my own life has taught me. The rest is based on observing other people's lives. Some of the lessons have been beautiful, whereas others have been tough. I have made mistakes and I have learned. I have known love and pain, disappointment and success – and I am sure there is still much ahead of me, more to learn from and more to make me grow.

I don't know how old you are as you read the parts of this book that interest you. Age does not matter. What matters is whether the words touch your heart in the way I hope they will. The 'voice' in italics at the beginning of some of the chapters is the voice of several daughters, including my own. As you read, it is my hope that the pages will provide you with inspiration and some alternative ways of approaching life's challenges.

Part One

Life Skills

1 Communication

'Communicate. It's easy to say, not always so easy to do. I sometimes wish the person I'm with could just read my mind. Why is it so difficult sometimes?'

Communication is the key ingredient in a relationship and without it a relationship cannot work. Lack of communication can even kill it. And trying to revive it will take much more effort than if you'd paid attention in the first place. Whether the relationship is between you and your friends, your family, a teacher, a work colleague or anyone else you need to interact with, if you don't communicate well it won't work well.

> 'Communication keeps relationships alive and thriving'

We're often very poor listeners – and listening is a key element in communication. We may think we listen, but we often don't hear what a person is really saying. Also, in spite of all the talking we do, we're often poor at sharing our true feelings.

How well do you listen?

Do you encourage the people you have a relationship with to talk to you? Do you really listen to them? Listening not only allows you to know people, it is also a sign of respect – respect for them and their feelings. Pick your closest three relationships and see how accurately you can answer these questions (without asking the people involved first):

- What is their biggest dream in life?
- What makes them really happy?
- What are their biggest fears?
- What achievement are they most proud of?
- Do they have any spiritual beliefs?

☀ What makes them laugh or cry?

☀ What is their favourite food, music or type of film?

☀ What are the important issues going on in their lives right now?

☀ Who are their closest friends?

☀ What are their important needs, socially, physically and emotionally?

☀ Would they be able to accurately answer these questions about you?

These are examples of the information we share with each other when we communicate. Communication is as much about sharing as about listening and it takes some effort to be good at both. Communication can also be verbal or non-verbal, but I am focusing here on the verbal side.

What makes a good communicator?

Concentrating on a few specific elements can make a significant difference to the way we communicate and to the level of success we achieve. The key elements are:

☀ **Being genuinely interested in the other person** and in what makes him or her 'tick'. By wanting to understand this person's thoughts, opinions, joys, fears and dreams, we build the links we need for a satisfying relationship.

☀ **Being a good listener** and paying attention to what the other person is saying without being distracted. Acknowledging what we have heard and drawing the person out to tell us more opens up the channels of communication.

☀ **Responding to what the person has said** and then, at the appropriate time, sharing your own thoughts, feelings and experiences.

☀ **Thinking before you speak**. A rash word, once spoken, can't be taken back and sometimes it's best to say less and to listen more.

Communication is a two-way street and it requires genuine interest from both parties. Sometimes the listening may happen at one time and the sharing at another – they don't always have to happen together.

Observations have been made through the ages that girls (and women) often find deep verbal communication easier than boys do. They tend to share their feelings more easily, particularly with other girls, and enjoy swapping their stories, experiences, loves, fears and dreams. Many boys (but certainly not all) tend to focus on communicating the more practical, factual aspects of life around them and spend less time on delving into the emotional and analytical aspects. This can lead, especially in adult life, to misunderstandings and discord in relationships, particularly if one person delights in extensive two-way interaction and the other is uncommunicative.

Being aware of the importance of good communication is crucial to developing and sustaining effective and harmonious relationships, within your family, school, work and other environments.

People who don't communicate well

People who aren't communicating well may find themselves:

✳ Not listening because they switch off when someone else is speaking.
✳ Being bored by anything anyone else has to say. They often have definite opinions about most topics and others' opinions don't really count.
✳ Being quick to jump to conclusions about what the other person is trying to say and not giving him or her the time to say it.
✳ Talking non-stop. They go on for hours, not noticing that other people may want to say something or that there's no more interest from them.
✳ Getting into too much detail. They'll be telling a story and each point reminds them of a sub-story. Eventually the listener loses the plot and switches off.

It can be hard if you're a 'communicator' at heart and you have a relationship with someone who isn't. But don't give up trying because that will make matters worse. Do your best to get the person to see the importance of communication, even if it means seeking advice or buying them a book which explains it. Keep trying, for the sake of the relationship. It's worth the effort if it works out.

The benefits of good communication

Making an effort to be a good communicator benefits you throughout your life in the following ways:

☀ You'll be liked by others and they'll seek your company.

☀ Doors will open for you and you may get opportunities you wouldn't normally have.

☀ Your relationships will be deeper, happier and stronger.

☀ One day, in a relationship with someone you love, there will be closeness, understanding and plenty to talk about.

☀ Problems can be resolved as they arise instead of being buried and then silently growing.

☀ You'll know a lot more about what's going on around you.

☀ Life will be easier and more enjoyable in a number of ways.

☀ You will experience greater fulfilment and happiness.

Communication keeps relationships alive and thriving. Cultivate it; it's an investment in your happiness!

2 Passion

Passion is what makes the world go around. Passion is the ingredient that turns mediocrity into fireworks. Let yourself feel it in your heart. If you feel strongly about something, let that feeling grow until it burns within you, until you're moved to act or speak out.

A positive force

Passion can move mountains. It can energise your life and your whole experience of yourself. It can mobilise you to take up a cause you feel strongly about. Life is too short and too special to waste on half-hearted feelings and vague enthusiasm. Let me stress that I am talking here about the passion that ignites positive feelings and actions. You should give no time to any form of 'passion' that is applied negatively, as violence or to cause harm to anyone or anything. That kind of passion is usually just an excuse to vent uncontrolled feelings of anger.

> 'Passion is what turns mediocrity into fireworks'

Passion is a feeling that can work for you throughout your life. People who go through life with their eyes half shut and their enthusiasm levels just above freezing will never be half as happy or fulfilled as they could be. Their lives may be calmer, but they'll never know indescribable joy and fervent excitement. They won't tremble with anticipation, cry for someone else's sorrow or dance their heart out for love.

Girls often find themselves consumed by passions such as horses, ballet, animal rights, film stars, music, the Internet, and various other interests. Such passions can bring a high degree of involvement with and knowledge of the particular topic and can serve as a platform for gathering further information. It is, however, important to keep the level of interest in perspective so that it doesn't become an obsession.

Being passionate about something is good, but becoming obsessed clouds your thinking and eventually brings about negative results, so make sure that you're aware of the difference and that you maintain a balanced approach.

Passion in a relationship is what inspires many films and books. It's what makes the Earth move for you. But it's not good if it's the only aspect of a relationship. You do need all the other aspects described in chapter 15, on Relationships, but passion sure makes things exciting.

When you feel passionately about a topic, event or injustice, that's when your creative juices start to flow. That's when you suddenly feel inspiration and energy surge through you and that's when you are best able to take the action you want to.

It's good to know that you're alive. Don't just survive life. Live it, feel it and taste it the way it can be. Keep love at the core of all your actions and go out and live!

3 What does it take to succeed?

'We were given a fund-raising project to test our creativity and entrepreneurial skills. I drew up a great scheme which involved making fudge and cakes on order. I gave out flyers to all the parents and got orders, but then it all got too confused and complicated and I lost money instead of making it. All that effort and the project still failed…'

Obviously not everyone can succeed every time, but it's interesting to observe the differences in approach between those people who consistently succeed and those who just as consistently fail.

There's a saying that 'success breeds success', and it's been proven time and again. My work has given me the opportunity to study many people and their approaches, and I quickly realised that there is a definite set of guidelines which, if followed, dramatically increases your chance of achieving success. This 'formula' for success becomes clear as soon as you observe the methods used and the approach taken by consistent achievers. Whether it has to do with school work, projects, extra-mural interests or your career, this formula can be very applicable and valuable.

Ten keys to success

If you want to succeed at whatever you undertake, you need to follow these key aims:

1 **Set goals for yourself.** Let yourself dream and don't be afraid to aim high. Then plan how you will go about getting to where you want to be. It's good to do a reality check to make sure your goal is achievable and then, if you're satisfied, start to visualise it so vividly that it becomes quite tangible for you. Picture the end result, picture your success and then picture the actions you need to take.

2 **Be determined and work hard**. Be prepared to work towards your goal with unwavering diligence and focus. If it gets too difficult, set yourself some mini-goals in between and achieve them first. Do your best at all times, set high standards and remind yourself that if something is worth doing, it's worth doing well – and it's also worth finishing. If you realise that you're at a disadvantage due to a lack of skills or information, plan how you will obtain what you need.

3 **Be well organised**. Being organised is essential as it dramatically increases your effectiveness and simultaneously reduces your stress levels. To be well organised you need good self-discipline, sound time-management skills and an up-to-date list of all your tasks, their importance rating and due dates.

4 **Attitude, attitude, attitude**. Having a good attitude is irreplaceable when it comes to succeeding in your endeavours. (Chapter 5 on attitude, outlines some of the key aspects.)

5 **Make sure you can 'sleep soundly at night'**. Don't get involved in anything that isn't right, and if you are thinking of taking a dishonest short-cut, don't. Avoid knocking the competition: succeed through your efforts and not by taking someone down.

6 **Develop good social and communication skills**. Most undertakings require an ability to build relationships and to promote ideas and results (verbally and in writing). The better you come across, the more convincing you will be and the more impact you will have on those you interact with. Listening ability is also integral as it enables you to gather information and ideas as well as helping you to identify needs and forge relationships.

7 **Be prepared to take risks**. (If you don't get out of the boat you'll never know if you can walk on water.) Weigh the pros and cons, have the courage to venture into territory which may be foreign to you and don't be afraid to be different. Remember that innovation doesn't come from following the sheep.

8 **Have a good sense of humour.** See the funny side of life and don't take yourself too seriously.

9 **Don't be afraid to admit when you're wrong.** Learn the lessons from any setbacks you encounter and then move forward.

10 **Don't give up.** Success doesn't always come easily – you need plenty of perseverance.

So how do you rate on these points? Is there anything you feel you should work on improving? If there is, then work out a plan of what you need to do in order to improve and then check with yourself at regular intervals to see whether you're happy with your progress.

Something you also need to be aware of is that not everyone around you will always want you to succeed. Some people may feel that you're taking on something that, for example, girls don't 'typically' do, or they may be jealous of your achievements, or if you're dealing with people who are insecure they might try to put you down in the mistaken belief that this will make them look better. If you truly want to succeed then don't allow your aims to be undermined or deterred. Remain positive, focused and determined to achieve your maximum potential. You'll eventually show the sceptics, and yourself, that success is possible.

> 'Being organised increases effectiveness and reduces stress levels'

When success eludes you

If it should ever happen that you do put in an overwhelming and sustained effort, and still success eludes you, then it's a good idea to re-examine your goal to see if it really is realistic and achievable. Check to see whether you really did include all the 10 success-inducing ingredients, and if so, try to find out what could have prevented you from succeeding. If it seems that you are just not able to succeed, then have a look at Chapter 45, When You Don't Get What You Want, and then try to re-define your goals. Sometimes we are tripped up by unforeseen factors and we then have to adjust our direction accordingly.

To fully savour the satisfaction that success brings, it's important that you have a definition of what 'success' means for you in the task you're undertaking. Success can mean different things to different people, and if you don't define what it means for you, you could possibly miss the impact when it happens. Success can mean: passing an exam, or passing with an average greater than 80 per cent; being the best-liked member of a team; completing your project on time, within budget and with outstanding reviews; being chosen to play in a team, or being in the first team; earning well; being promoted ... . The list can go on and on, but it illustrates that success can be measured in different ways and it's important to know how you define it so that you'll recognise when you've achieved it. Go for it, believe in yourself and paint your success-filled future on the canvas of life!

4 Truth and honesty – how important are they?

'My friend Kelly asked me today if I liked her new haircut. I don't really – I think it's too short, but she always gets so upset if I say I don't like something about her, even when it's something unimportant, like hair. It will always grow back! Telling the truth can be hard! It's often one of the most difficult things to stick to.'

Truth is one of the most precious values we can grow within us. Truth – and trying to live a life based on truth – helps to make us the person we should be. So many things happen, we slip, we do something wrong – and we are afraid to admit it. But afraid of what? Of being punished or laughed at, ridiculed or rejected. If we are ridiculed or rejected, maybe those doing it to us are not worthy of our friendship? Maybe being true is more important than their acceptance.

Truth demands great strength of will from us – strength of will, of convictions, of character. That strength often fails us. Our human spirit weakens and lets us down. We take the path that's easier, the one of least resistance. Maybe the path that brings us more fun – in the short-term.

To give up truth is to become pliable and able to be influenced by anyone who shows more strength or influence over us.

It leads us in the wrong direction. It allows us to break down our values and ultimately leads us to loss of self-respect and of our strength of character. It's also scary how often one lie leads to another, how each lie starts to come more easily, and how the lies grow increasingly bigger as we continue. Before we know it, lying becomes a part of us and we forget how serious it is.

Truth, white lies and the dilemmas we encounter

We can often find ourselves in a dilemma when, for example, it comes to being asked for comments about how a friend looks or dresses or what others think of her boyfriend. There are times when it's hard to know what to say so as not to upset a close friend, and the debate about when to tell a 'harmless' white lie and when to tell the truth is unresolved.

Whenever you find yourself in one of these delicate situations it's important to be sensitive to the other person's feelings. Unless telling the truth will be unnecessarily and destructively painful, you should always be gently truthful. If you're in danger of causing uncalled-for pain,

> 'Once you accept small dishonesties they'll lead to bigger ones'

then it's best to evaluate the importance of the issue and then, if it really is the right thing to do, avoid comment. (I'm not saying here that you should lie, I'm saying that under certain conditions you could perhaps avoid making a comment, by changing the topic of conversation, for example.)

You do, however, need to be aware that in many cases sparing someone the truth can end up hurting them more in the long term. On the other hand, you also need to be aware of the effect of giving your opinion as it's quite possible that your thoughts about, for example, a friend's dress or hair are very subjective and if you don't happen to like it, it may not mean that it really deserves negative comment.

Truth – and judgement

You need to judge the importance of expressing or withholding your opinion, and about whether you ever feel that a 'white lie' is justified. A 'white lie' is one that results in no-one getting hurt and with no possible negative consequences, now or in the future. My advice is to tell the truth at all times, but you could occasionally find yourself in situations where you'll have to make a judgement call about what you're going to do.

If the issue you're facing is one concerning values, morals, someone's safety, ethical behaviour or other key elements, then choosing to remain silent is never a good decision. Many people prefer to remain silent to avoid conflict, confrontation or becoming involved, but if you believe that what you are being exposed to is wrong then it is essential that you find the courage to speak up, no matter what the consequences. Standing up for your convictions shows a strength of character which will inevitably stand you in good stead.

Situations that test your strength of character include those that involve exposing yourself to some kind of risk. It could be the risk of landing in trouble over something you (or someone else) did, or it could be the risk of losing a friendship or of alienating someone who asked you to ignore or keep secret some misdemeanour. Perhaps the guy you've fallen for tries to draw you into doing something illegal, and you know that by telling the truth you'll lose the chance of a relationship with him. Or you're about to go home from a party and you see that the driver is drunk, and you know that by speaking up you'll find yourself without a lift, and you may be ridiculed by the others for being a spoil-sport. No matter how hard it may be, there is no better alternative than to tell the truth in such situations.

Truth – and loyalty to the group

There are also going to be times when a sense of camaraderie may call on you to tell a lie in order to assume group-wide blame for a prank done by someone else. There is a film called *Scent of a Woman* which depicts so well the dilemma faced by the young sponsored student who witnesses a wicked prank carried out by a group of wealthy rebellious students. The principal knows that the student saw the culprits and gives him the choice of identifying the wrongdoers – or being expelled. The student chooses to remain silent and indicates that he is not prepared to betray fellow students, in spite of knowing that his choice will terminate all his chances of studying and qualifying. He makes a judgement call to be loyal to his colleagues, even if it comes at great cost to himself.

What would you have done in his position, where telling the truth would have meant being ostracised by your fellow students, and refraining from telling the truth risked everything you were working for? Fortunately for the student, the circumstances in the film changed and he was seen as a hero for displaying strong loyalty, whereas the culprits were humiliated. Had the circumstances not changed, his loyalty would have cost him dearly.

These types of situations bring home our vulnerability and the dilemmas in which we can so easily find ourselves. If you ever feel that you are in just such a quandary, ask yourself the questions listed in Chapter 51, Temptation, and then decide which course you truly believe is the right one, for the present and for the future.

Be strong, be true to yourself, stand your ground, stick to the truth, and be able to face yourself with love and pride.

Honesty: are there alternatives?

Is honesty a choice? Yes. You'll be making choices for the rest of your life and honesty is one of them. In today's world we're often presented with opportunities which are not honest and yet they may seem to be attractive: someone offers you a copy of tomorrow's exam paper; you find a purse containing money; a shop assistant makes a mistake and undercharges you; a waiter omits an item from your bill…

Take the honest way, every single time. You'll find that it makes your life much easier and much happier in the long term. If you're thinking to yourself that it's easier said than done, consider your alternatives. Is there a better solution?

Sometimes honesty takes guts. Sometimes it requires you to be strong. Temptation to ignore the honest way can be hard to resist at times, so the most effective solution is to establish honesty as one of your life's principles. Making honesty a non-negotiable part of your character gives you the strength to stick to it.

Why is being honest such a big deal? Because without it you lose yourself. Without it you can't tell right from wrong. You lose your values and your character. You become a person who is easily swayed by others, who will do anything they suggest even if it's obviously wrong. Once you accept small dishonesties these will inevitably lead to bigger ones, and then it's much harder to stop.

When you're being dishonest, eventually everything you do will become dishonest. It's like the slip described in When You've Made a Mistake, (Chapter 50). Once you slip on life's icy slope, unless you scramble up fast you'll slide further and further down.

If you think this is an exaggeration, look at the people now in jail. Other than those who are in for a spontaneous crime of violence, the rest are probably there because of some initial dishonesty. Their dishonesty no doubt started small and got out of hand. If you never allow dishonesty to enter your life you'll save yourself a whole lot of trouble and anguish. Honesty is called for in every situation you come across and especially in:

☀ all dealings where money is involved
☀ any agreements you make (verbal or written)
☀ handling others' possessions
☀ relationships
☀ studies
☀ work.

Temptation can wear disguises

Temptation sometimes disguises dishonesty as 'just something you want'. It can be borrowing money which you don't intend to return, helping yourself to school or company stationery, cheating in a test or a relationship, or omitting to tell the truth. (See Chapter 51 on Temptation, for more about this topic.)

For long-term happiness, recognise temptation when you feel it, stop in your tracks and choose the honest way. You're bound to trip along the way some time – we all do – but if your value is honesty it'll pick you up and put you back on the straight path. Be aware and take charge of yourself and your actions. You'll like yourself for it!

5 Your attitude makes you a winner

Your attitude is more important than your intellectual ability. A person with average ability and a brilliant attitude is more likely to succeed than a brilliant person with a bad attitude.

In my business career I've had the opportunity to study hundreds of success and failure cases. The one common factor to all those who are successful is their attitude. It doesn't matter how young or old you are, it's your attitude that makes the difference between success and mediocrity. It helps you to make it in life. It brings you happiness and friends. If it sounds a bit like a magic potion, that's because it is.

You can choose your attitude

Some of us are naturally more positive than others, but the good news is that we can choose the attitude we want. It's something we can have overnight.

The elements that contribute to having a good attitude include:

☀ **A positive approach**. If you have a cheerful and positive outlook towards others, tasks and life in general, then people will like to be around you.

☀ **Willingness to undertake whatever task is necessary**. Things don't just happen by themselves and the world needs doers.

☀ **Flexibility**. Being able to adapt to circumstances helps you cope better and makes you a more pleasant companion.

☀ **Reliability**. It's wonderful to deal with someone who, having undertaken to do something, always does it. This includes meeting deadlines and being on time for appointments.

☀ **Listening**. The world is full of talkers and it's a pleasure to find someone who is interested in others.

☀ **Searching for the solution**. When a problem presents itself, don't despair or say you can't do something because of it. Look for a way to resolve it.

☼ **Enthusiasm.** If you're enthusiastic you inspire others (and you enjoy life more).

☼ **Giving others the benefit of the doubt.**

☼ **Being able to laugh at yourself.**

You'll find that if you adopt a positive attitude then everything around you suddenly starts to look brighter, and all your interactions with people take on a more positive feel.

Some of us sometimes struggle with sudden swings in our mood and it's important to be aware of the effect that moodiness has on the people around us. No matter how justified you may feel in indulging your bad mood, it ultimately alienates everyone who has anything to do with you and results in your day being much worse than it could have been. At certain times of the month hormones can play havoc with your outlook and demeanour, and it is then that you need to be extra watchful and strict with yourself, and not allow yourself to succumb to moodiness. Hard as it may be during such times, practising self-control and actively focusing on being positive can make a huge difference to you and those around you.

'Your attitude makes the difference between success and mediocrity'

A good attitude is priceless. It really can change your life for the better. Even when things are tough, it's your attitude that helps you overcome and survive them. It's magic, it's free and it's yours if you want it!

6 When you want to be liked

Recently I talked to Sandy, a 16-year-old girl whose family had moved to a new town and found herself struggling to make friends. She said that she didn't know what to do to be liked. This sparked off a long and interesting debate and eventually, having looked at all the aspects we could think of, this is what we came up with:

☀ Know who you are and what you believe in – and then be yourself.
☀ Know what you like, strive for truth, integrity and justice – and be strong.
☀ Always do your best, be honest, and pick friends who share your values.
☀ Identify your priorities. Sometimes being liked won't come first.

There are also some specific points that we agreed are important and we summarised them like this:

☀ **Show people that you genuinely care for them.**
☀ **Be friendly.** Be warm, affectionate and compassionate.
☀ **Smile a lot.** A smile melts barriers and establishes an instant connection between people.
☀ **Be humble.** Let others discover your talents for themselves and they'll do the bragging for you.
☀ **Be assertive, firm, yet gentle.** Know what you are striving for and know the boundaries you set yourself.
☀ **Be helpful.** Look for opportunities to be of help where needed.
☀ **Have a positive and cheerful attitude to everything in life.** Don't be moody. It's amazing what results you can achieve with a positive approach.
☀ **Listen well.** People like someone who is interested in them and you'll learn a lot more than if you do all the talking.

☀ **Be considerate**. Think about your actions and the effect they have.

☀ **Be a good judge of timing**. Identify the appropriate time for asking, for seeking attention, being witty or loud – and the time for waiting, for being patient or quiet.

☀ **Don't let yourself be too spoilt**. If you're cute or clever, some people will 'spoil' you, and if you let it go to your head it won't make you popular.

☀ **Have good manners**. Your manners (or lack of them) say a lot about you. A person with good manners is always welcome. Anyone with bad manners comes across as selfish or spoilt and is not a pleasure to be with. The first eight points in Manners, Chapter 8, have some useful tips.

☀ **Look for the fun aspects in your environment** and enjoy them, and yourself. Being happy and full of the joys of life draws others to you like a magnet.

☀ **Be sociable**, and invite people to come over to your place for a meal or some fun activity, such as watching a film, listening to music or playing a game. If you can cook, that's great. If you can't, then get pizza, but find opportunities to entertain people in a relaxed way. Then you'll get to know each other better.

It's important to remember that life is about choices. The behaviour you choose will influence how others see you and react to you.

We had that conversation a few months ago, and Sandy came bounding in the other day saying that focusing on these points definitely works. In addition to the reactions of those around her, both young and old, she also likes herself more too.

Do you really have to be 'popular'?

When you find yourself consciously wanting to be liked, it's a good idea to distinguish between being 'liked' and being 'popular'. Girls often judge themselves by how popular they are and this can result in losing their sense of self. Popularity, if it's based mostly on what others can get from being around you, can be very temporary and is often more about the others than about you. Genuine liking leads to true and lasting friendships, and brings far more long-term satisfaction.

If you find yourself suddenly thrown into a new environment, such as a new school or university, city or country (Chapter 54, Feeling Lonely or Alone, deals with some of the feelings that could come up), then being liked and making friends takes on more significance. Try not to get too stressed if the process seems to be taking longer than you'd expected and focus on getting on with your life. The 'liking' will happen – and friendships will develop and grow in due course.

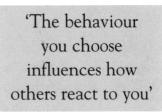

'The behaviour you choose influences how others react to you'

May all this help you in your life, now and later. It comes with the wish that your life will be filled with loving people who like you, respect you and care for you.

7 Let's talk

Most mothers throughout the world would like to say to their daughters: 'Talk to me … when something is on your mind, when something troubles you, when you have something to share, when you want to celebrate.

'I am always interested in sharing with you whatever is going through your mind and your heart. If you want my opinion, tell me. If you just want me to listen – I'll do that too. Even if it's something really shocking, try me! I may not always agree with your point of view or your behaviour. I may have different ideas about some things, but overall I've probably shared very similar needs, problems, desires, pains and joys.

'Tell me the things you'd like me to know, things you'd like me to do or not do. If you don't tell me, I can't know. I might even jump to incorrect conclusions.

> 'Communication is the fabric that holds people together'

'Sometimes we can talk by writing to each other, sometimes just by sitting quietly together. If it seems that I'm too busy, stop me in my tracks, because above all I want to hear you.

'There may be times when we might find it difficult to talk, even when we know that we need to. Asking questions, drawing each other's thoughts about related aspects, and sharing past experiences can help to get conversation flowing, thus paving the way to talking about the important present issues.

'Communication is so precious, it's the fabric that holds people together, so let's weave this precious gift and let it bind us together forever. Whenever we can, let's talk.'

8 Manners

'Manners maketh man', goes the old saying. It's so true. This may be the 21st century, but your manners still say a great deal about you. They open doors of opportunity for you and, if your manners are displeasing, they can close them.

Some manners are seen as being essential and others as 'nice touches'. The ones I'm about to mention are those you may find most useful. You probably do most of these things anyway, but the following lists can be a handy reminder.

The 'essential eight'

❋ **Greetings and goodbyes**: expressing warmth and enthusiasm shows people we're happy to see them.

❋ **Show respect to elderly people**. Let them through a door first, offer them refreshments, seat them comfortably and keep an eye out for dangerous steps. These are all signs of respect.

❋ **Mealtime etiquette**. Sit properly and hold the knife and fork correctly. Wait for others to serve themselves first, check to see that there is enough to go around and politely ask for something you don't have or that is not within easy reach. Don't monopolise the conversation. Show appreciation for the food and, if something isn't to your liking, ask for very little. Say thanks after every meal (even at home).

❋ **Please and thank you**. Remember that these are powerful words.

❋ **Offer to help**. Offer to help when others are busy with something.

❋ **Show respect** towards friends' parents (and your parents' friends too).

❋ **When in someone's house**, ask before taking food or drinks, even if they know you well – it's polite.

❋ **Show enthusiasm** and gratitude when receiving a gift. If you can't give thanks in person, then it's good to write a note.

The 'nice touches'

☀ When you're in company, avoid long and loud conversations on your mobile. And don't spend time texting when you're with others – it makes them feel you are more interested in your phone than them.

☀ If you're running late to meet someone, phone to let them know.

☀ Pay compliments. If you're thinking something nice about someone, by saying it you'll brighten their day.

☀ When staying as a guest, bring your hosts a gift, clean the bath, make the bed and keep the room tidy. Afterwards, write them a thank-you note.

☀ When eating out, pay for your share unless it's quite clear that you've been invited out. If you're invited out, return the favour sometime.

☀ When going to friends for a meal, bring a small gift (eg flowers or chocolates) and thank them again the following day.

☀ Be polite to anyone providing a service. If the service is unsatisfactory it's best to point it out and then report it to a superior. Losing your cool and exploding, even if you have been wronged, will seldom achieve the required result. Stay composed and clearly state your dissatisfaction – it is far more effective.

It's important to remember that manners vary according to culture, so it's a good idea to inform yourself about what's expected wherever you find yourself. What's polite in one culture may well be seen as rude in another.

> 'Your manners say a great deal about you'

It's a fact of life that people like the company of those who have good manners and are a pleasure to be with. Bad manners can seriously embarrass you, as well as brand you as inconsiderate and disrespectful. Good manners are remembered long after you've gone.

9 Being a teenager

'Why is it that so much is written about teenagers and so many jokes are made about how difficult they can be? It's like we're suddenly aliens or something, speaking a different language from the people we've shared our lives with until that moment.'

Well, life really does seem to change around the age of 13. For some girls it's just a greater awareness of growing up and maturing. For others it can bring much frustration and even anguish and pain. This time of changing from a girl to an adult can be hard for you and for us, the parents. Each of us thinks that what we're feeling is unique and it's easy to forget about the others in the family.

Why is it so hard for teenagers?

It's hard because two things happen: one, you really are 'growing up', you're more aware of yourself, the way you are, the person you'd like to be, your needs, your fears and your growing independence; and two, you may find that we, your parents, don't seem to understand the changes in you. You may feel that you're still being treated like the child you once were and you may suddenly feel as if you are on the opposite side of a fence to your parents.

Other things can happen which make things even harder for you. Any time of change is scary, even when you're much older, because you don't know what's waiting for you. When all these things start to happen it can all be hard to handle.

☀ You're changing, but you may not know which way you want to go.
☀ Your biggest fear is rejection. You want to feel accepted by your peers and you're never quite sure what they really think of you.
☀ You watch your friends and you may want to model yourself on those

you think are the way you'd like to be. You can sometimes be disappointed with the outcome.

✸ You may at times feel pressure from your group of friends to be a certain way or do things they do even though this may not feel right to you.

✸ You want to be your own individual and yet others' opinions count a great deal.

✸ At school you're loaded with an increasing volume of work and pressure to perform. It often feels as if it's too much and you won't cope.

✸ Your social life becomes steadily more important, with many invitations to hang out with your friends. You want to go out whenever asked and you can't understand why your parents ask questions about where you're going and with whom, and why the brakes are sometimes applied, accompanied by requests to spend time with your family.

✸ Your mood may sometimes swing from feeling upbeat and confident to insecure and unhappy. This is scary, and because you don't understand the reason you may react with frustration or aggression. There are times when you really cannot understand your reactions and it's almost as if there's another person hiding inside you. The hormonal changes in you can send you on an unpredictable roller-coaster ride of emotions and sensitivities.

✸ Your body is also changing – sometimes you'll like it, sometimes it may worry you. You'll probably also be aware that you're changing faster than many of the boys in your age group.

✸ When someone (especially your parents) challenges you, you may show anger or become sulky, moody or just plain obstinate. This only makes things worse and you might feel that you're caught in a no-win situation.

✸ You experience an awakening of and increase in sexual feelings.

✸ You may feel that you're not a child anymore and yet you're not an adult. Who are you and what should you be doing, feeling, saying…?

I'm not saying that you definitely will feel all the things I've described, but you may feel some of them.

Why is this stage hard for parents?

Because, in spite of our many years of acquired wisdom, we too are thrown by change. We may not understand it or we may feel threatened by it. We may also be confused by this young person who was and always will be our child, who is changing before our eyes and who sometimes does things that worry us. We're sometimes frightened that you're growing up too fast and that you want to tackle things you're not yet ready for. We're also very aware that we need to acknowledge your transition to adulthood and that we need to offer you greater responsibility while simultaneously providing the stability, guidance and support you need.

The dreaded 'generation gap'

If you suddenly start to like things that we, your parents, may not, such as different music, weird clothes, going to strange clubs and hanging out with certain friends, this is the time you may experience what's been labelled the 'generation gap'. This gap will worsen if you get involved in something that clashes with our value system, such as smoking, drinking, drugs or sex. We won't understand how this could have happened, we may start to despair and we may become angry. You might be trying only to prove a point, but you will feel rejected by our reaction and so you may try to assert yourself further by rebelling more. It turns into a vicious circle which spirals down, resulting in everyone involved feeling very unhappy.

Is there a solution?

The one essential ingredient in all happy relationships is communication. During your teenage years, more than ever, it is vital to work hard at keeping the communication channels open with your parents. It is something that you, as well as the whole family, must remember.

By communication I mean: sharing your feelings, your fears, your dreams, your experiences – and really listening to what other people have to say. When we talk openly to each other and when we are genuinely interested in what is said, then we can discuss what's happening, the differences we may be having and the frustrations we feel. For communication to really work you need to mix it with love and a mutual willingness to arrive at win-win solutions.

Discussing your feelings openly can be scary. You're making yourself vulnerable and that means you could be hurt. So what's the alternative? Shutting yourself in, making it impossible for anyone else to understand what's happening inside you, feeling sorry for yourself, misunderstood, alienated, alone, hurt and angry?

If you want a really good relationship with your family, there is no alternative to loving communication. If your mother doesn't know what you're feeling or thinking, how can she know what you need or want from her? How can she be of any help or support? All that will happen is the gap will widen and both of you will retreat to your corners feeling hurt and frustrated.

> 'It's almost as if there's another person hiding inside of you'

Parents have feelings too

This may be an obvious statement, but it's easy to forget. We are the ones who are supposed to know everything and you're the one facing the challenges of growing up. We ought to be always consistent, calm, secure, able to take any abuse without flinching and filled with unwavering wisdom. Unfortunately it's not like that. We too are human. We make mistakes. We're also afraid of rejection. We too have insecurities and doubts.

We often wish we knew more and that we were better able to put theory into practice, but we have our limitations and we must work within them. We do, however, love you more than words can describe. Our love for you is at the centre of everything we do. We want the best for you and whatever we do is with that intention. We want you to grow up happy and confident. We want you to walk a straight path, with the courage to stick to your convictions.

We also have fears and we often worry. We worry about your safety and your wellbeing. We're sometimes afraid of what it'll be like when one day you have your own life and you're gone from our home. We know this sounds selfish, but it's hard to know that a person who has been the centre of our lives for so long will soon step out into the wide world to set up her own independent life, with her own interests and priorities, possibly living far away.

I'm sharing this with you not to make you feel guilty about your growing independence, but for you to understand why, as parents, we may sometimes seem overprotective or stupidly anxious about you. Looking at things from our perspective and reminding us to look at them from yours will help us all to understand things better.

Some helpful pointers

As you journey through your different stages of life and development you'll face new, unexpected and varied challenges. Some of the following pointers may be helpful:

※ Try not to let yourself be pushed off the path of truth and of doing the right thing.

※ If you make a mistake, see it, admit it, learn from it and then move forward to correct it. Don't be afraid to share it with someone close – two heads are better than one and someone's love for you makes them a creative problem-solver.

※ Don't be overwhelmed by the challenges you face. See them as opportunities for learning and growth.

※ Remember that your maturity grows when you accept responsibility.

※ Hanging out with 'good' people helps you stay firmly on the right path. There's much wisdom in the saying: 'You become the company you keep.'

※ Treat others the way you would like to be treated.

※ Self-control is important. It builds strength and helps you cope with life's curved balls.

※ Learn from the past, don't dwell on it. Live for today and do your best. Look forward to tomorrow, don't fear it.

Your teenage years are the transition between the child you're outgrowing and the adult you're becoming. Enjoy them, savour them and let yourself exhilarate in all the new feelings and experiences you will encounter.

10 Why do values bring happiness?

'My friends say that values are old-fashioned and that life is more fun if you don't have to worry about rules or guidelines. Why does it work for some, whilst others are so unhappy?'

Values provide your life with a backbone. Without them you might temporarily feel more flexible and free, but at some point your life is bound to collapse in a heap. Like backbones, values provide a central structure which helps to keep us together. Sometimes they may feel as if they restrict us and our yearning for freedom may cause us to throw them away, but we soon feel the impact of their absence.

❀ What are 'values'?

Some of the values and approaches to life which can affect our lives include:

※ Telling the truth.
※ Being trustworthy.
※ Honesty and integrity (includes not stealing or cheating).
※ Respecting life, i.e. not killing.
※ Sticking to your word and your promise.
※ Having respect for laws and rules.
※ Honouring your commitments.
※ Taking responsibility for your actions.
※ Showing respect to parents, elders and people in authority.
※ Sticking to your principles in spite of peer-pressure to do otherwise.
※ Avoiding gossiping about or criticising others.
※ Focusing on being kind, sincere and compassionate.
※ Staying faithful in a relationship.
※ Spiritual beliefs which guide our actions.

☀ Not taking part in something which could harm your body, your life, or someone else.
☀ Avoiding promiscuous behaviour.
☀ Treating others the way you would like to be treated.
☀ Approaching all tasks with diligence.

These are just some of the many 'value-based' guidelines which people adopt to help steer them through life. You'll no doubt come up with many others.

A life without values

Some people go through life without paying attention to such values. They prefer to opt for 'freedom' from any guidelines which might prove restrictive and they hope for an easier life. Admittedly, a life without values can sometimes seem quite appealing. We don't have to answer to anyone, we're unrestrained by frustrating rules and laws, we can act without worrying about hurting others, and we can make sure that we always come first. We can take what we want, tell lies when we need to, be violent, uncaring, swear, steal, cheat on our relationships, and possibly even kill someone inconvenient to us, whenever we feel so inclined.

A bit of an exaggeration? Not necessarily. Without values there's nothing to stop us, is there? We choose to have no boundaries and no self-discipline, so we're free. Free to do anything we please. And that freedom can take us to all sorts of unexpected places, even ones we never envisaged. Oh, what fun!

Great fun – until life starts to dish us up with some of what we've been dishing out to others. When we suddenly find ourselves on the receiving end of selfishness, dishonesty, cruelty or betrayal, then it's no longer such fun. And if we're caught for breaking the law then all 'fun' vanishes instantly. When the tables are turned we quickly begin to be unhappy with the state of things. We might feel that life is unfair, we're unlucky, people are picking on us, we're misunderstood, deprived of opportunities, deceived, or victimised. We start to blame others for our mess, and we can become angry, bitter and resentful. We might start to seek revenge on our perceived tormentors, our self-respect crumbles, we don't trust anyone, we make ever more mistakes, and so the cycle starts to entrap us.

Suddenly life is no longer as happy as it was meant to be. Suddenly this 'freedom' we yearned for has become a prison from which we cannot escape. And then what? Where do we go from here? We are, as always, faced with choices. We can consider opting for a life based on values, or we can continue to avoid values with grim determination.

Values are your guiding markers

Much as people might rebel against boundaries, and they might say that sticking to guidelines is boring, a life without them can easily lead to becoming lost. Having values is like using a map to help you navigate through life. Values are the markers which guide you onto the right path, and they help to keep you there. Whenever you're in doubt about how you should tackle a particular situation, refer to those markers.

We'll all wander off our chosen path at some stage and we'll sometimes find ourselves in trouble. Life will also inevitably throw curve-balls our way and they might fill us with

> 'Values give your life a backbone'

fear, discouragement, crisis, sorrow or doubt. At such times, it's what we do next that determines our future. And the values we have help us to decide how we'll tackle our next step. They steer us around some of life's potholes. So, whatever the circumstances, the more values we have and the better we stick to them, the better the long-term results will be.

Gradually, the more we rely on them, the more our values will help to ensure that our life becomes filled with peace, wisdom, love, contentment, and ultimately a new-found freedom. So, boring or inconvenient they might sometimes appear, but values certainly make life a lot easier!

11 Useful tips about life

'Sometimes I feel my life is like running an obstacle race, with hurdles to leap over, muddy puddles to cross and stony slopes to scramble up, and soon something is going to trip me up. I wish I had a Cheat's Guide to Life to make things easier.'

Look at life from all angles, peer beneath the stones that lie along your path to see what hidden surprises they may hold, and ponder about the secrets to happiness and the reasons why people do the things they do. This will allow you to navigate more easily through life.

Knowing the little tips that make life easier is like having the clues in a treasure hunt. It doesn't guarantee you'll always find the treasure, but it gives you guidance, an insight into what's involved and it makes the journey more fun. Getting lost can be frustrating or scary, especially when others race on ahead.

Little 'wisdoms'

Here's a collection of some of the little 'wisdoms' I've gathered:

※ Sometimes it's the little things in life that give the biggest pleasures – a beautiful sunset, a friend's smile, a walk in the fields.
※ Your approach to life determines so many of your life's experiences.
※ You can't always choose the situation you're in, but you can always choose how you're going to respond to it.
※ Respect yourself and others will respect you.
※ To give love to others you have to love yourself first.
※ Don't take anything for granted. It may not be there tomorrow.
※ Things don't happen without effort. If you want something, make it happen.
※ Angels pop up in unexpected places. Sometimes, just when you're in

need of something, someone appears with the very thing.

☀ Happiness sometimes surprises us when we stop trying too hard to find it.

☀ Resist the urge to gossip about others.

☀ Learn something new (not studies or job related) on a regular basis. It makes you and your life more interesting.

☀ Smile often. It brings you closer to people. It also prompts your brain to release more 'happy chemicals'.

☀ Take photos of all trips and special occasions. Every time you look at them you'll relive the experience.

☀ Indulge yourself regularly – with a candle-lit bubble bath, your favourite film, a walk in the park, a slice of cake…Whatever it is, it will remind you that you're special and worth a treat.

☀ Do things for those who are less fortunate than you. You'll bring them a ray of sunshine and their happiness will boomerang back into your life.

☀ Write a list of 50 things you want to do in your lifetime. Tick them off as you do them.

☀ Learn to change a tyre. You never know when it might save you.

☀ Learn to change a light-bulb and a plug; it might be your only chance of light some day.

☀ Change is an unavoidable part of life, so accept it with an open mind. Fighting change will lead to fighting yourself.

☀ Read many different books; they open up new worlds for you.

☀ Judge yourself by the person you are when no-one is looking.

☀ Cherish your femininity. Every now and again try new make-up, style your hair, do your nails and dress in something pretty – you'll feel beautiful!

☀ Know who you are. The better you define your values and what you stand for, the better your resistance against falling for what is bad for you.

☀ Start and end your day with a thought about the good things in your life.

☀ Develop your spiritual side. It will add a new dimension to your life.

☀ Timing is important. There's a time to speak and a time to keep quiet. Always know which time it is.

☼ Allow yourself to fall in love. Even if it ends at least you would have experienced the elation of loving.

☼ Life is not always about having what you want, it's also about wanting what you have.

> 'Knowing the little tips that make life easier is like having the clues in a treasure hunt'

☼ Write your eulogy (what you'd like said about your whole life). Then plan how you're going to live your life to make it come true.

☼ Half the fun of getting somewhere is the journey – savour every moment.

These little 'wisdoms' may smooth some of the path ahead of you and may contribute to your life being richer and more fulfilling.

12 You don't have to be perfect

'I sometimes don't like myself, I don't like the person I am. I feel boring, I don't like the way I sound or look, and I feel very stupid.'

Life is not about chastising yourself for not being perfect. Doing your best and striving to improve your best, that's what counts. If you expect yourself (and others) to be perfect you'll be disappointed. It does not mean that you should stop trying and that you should settle for mediocrity. Not at all. It just means that there's another way of looking at how you can be.

I'm the first one to urge you to do your best. If you do something, do it well. Aim as high as you can and put your whole effort into getting there. We've all been given talents and it's our duty to make sure we use them. Think of talent as a muscle. If you don't use it, it'll wither away and you'll even forget you have it. The more you use it the stronger it becomes. Perfection in your work is like that. Striving for top-quality, error-free work is something you should always do and it will earn you the recognition you deserve. If, however, you start to obsess about perfection, that's when you need to take a look at yourself.

Because we're human, we will never be perfect. We make mistakes. We must strive to make as few mistakes as possible, but at some point we'll inevitably still make some. It's what

> 'Talent is like a muscle, if you don't use it it'll wither away'

we do about those mistakes that's important. It's also the lessons we can learn from what happened that we should focus on. Life is an adventure made up of a string of experiences that teach us something each time. As long as we learn the lessons, avoid making the same mistakes again and improve ourselves as we go, then we're heading in the right direction.

In the school environment girls often judge perfection in themselves, and in others, by their school marks and by who becomes prefect, monitor or head-girl. Good marks are important, and it is essential to do one's best, but beyond that there are other aspects which are as important, and marks should not become an obsession and the only measure which counts. Sometimes the girls who score straight As in school end up doing little with their lives, whereas those who get Bs end up running companies. It's important to focus on more than one dimension, as Chapter 5 on Success outlines.

Beating yourself up for not being perfect is not only counter-productive, but it can also be a good excuse for not going further. If you give up on yourself you don't have to try anymore. So rather accept that you're not perfect, and then make a plan of how you can get around your weaknesses and how you can develop every last drop of your potential.

13 Lighten up – you'll float more easily

'You often tell me not to be so serious. What's wrong with being serious? I don't always feel like laughing. Sometimes the things you find funny I think are just silly.'

I mean don't let life weigh you down. Let yourself see the good bits and focus on them for a balanced experience. We so often let life turn us into serious people. It can happen quite easily, but if you're aware of the symptoms you can prevent them from taking a grip. I'm not talking here about merely taking your responsibilities seriously. That's very good and commendable. No, I'm referring to those times when you suddenly become serious or morose in your whole outlook and demeanour. Girls often encounter such heaviness of spirit during adolescence and many women live their entire lives weighed down by life and its inevitable demands.

What's wrong with being 'heavy'?
This is what's wrong with being 'heavy', for a start:

☀ As your life's challenges become more difficult, you may grow to be serious and even sombre. You may feel as if you're labouring under a heavy weight and you may no longer enjoy living life the way you were meant to.

☀ Seriousness and heaviness are contagious. The people around you will gradually seem to be more serious too. Usually this will apply only to their dealings with you and they'll still be bouncy towards others, but if you're in a bad way then they may catch it badly too.

☀ You look at life differently. Each new task may seem like a burden to you. You may appreciate its importance, but you won't be greeting it with open arms. You'll even tend to notice all the bad news in the papers and on TV and you'll overlook the good-news stories. You may be an authority on crime statistics, global warming, poverty or the cost of living, but you may not know about medical breakthroughs or other good news taking place around the world.

☀ You can catch your own 'disease' and you may grow increasingly heavier until you feel as if you're heading right down. No-one wants to be around someone who is permanently glum, and you could well find that your morose state of mind really does create an environment which will truly depress you.

The antidote to all this heavy stuff is to lighten up.

Ways to lighten up

I know it's easier said than done, but there are some things you can do:

☀ **Look for the funny side of life**. See the humour in some of life's everyday situations. It may only be, as happened to me recently, a car that aggressively overtook me going downhill and then proceeded to struggle up the next hill, steaming and backfiring as it wheezed along. While overtaking it I began to laugh and suddenly the whole day was much brighter. Actively seek out something which could be seen in a funny light and you'll be surprised at what you might find.

☀ **Shift your mindset**. This can take some practice, but you can do it. Tell yourself that you're going to lighten up and let yourself see more than just one way of looking at the circumstances you're in. Pick the most positive interpretation and run with that.

☀ **Laugh more**. Look for activities and occasions that will make you laugh. You can rent a DVD or see a film featuring a good comedy. You can scan book reviews and get a book which is rated as funny. You can go to watch a stand-up comedian or a funny play. You can even play a game with your dog or cat if you have one. Its exuberance and joyful antics will make any heaviness hard to maintain.

☀ **Act crazy sometimes**. This doesn't mean that you turn into a crackpot or do something dangerous, it just means occasionally letting your inhibitions go. If it means dressing funny and dancing around the room with your cat, then do it. If your friends watch in amazement, explain to them why you're doing it and don't let them put you off. The important assumption here is that you're not going to do something that feels wrong to you or that can hurt someone else. What I'm referring to is a bit of innocent fun which up to now you may have avoided due to shyness or 'heaviness'.

☀ **Stop being a worrier**. As long as you've done your best, things won't improve if you worry more about them. Playing the 'what if' game can also be very stressful. What if you don't pass? What if he doesn't call? What if they won't like it? All this eventually drains you of energy. Do your best, handle your responsibilities and then

> 'Worrying is like stepping into a blob of chewing gum – it goes with you everywhere and keeps interfering'

relax and focus on other things. Worrying is like stepping into a big blob of chewing gum. It goes with you everywhere you go and keeps interfering with what you're doing. Scrape it off and leave it behind.

☀ **Change your routine**. Get up a bit earlier, take a different route to school or work, once a week eat a new food you wouldn't normally consider and occasionally try on clothes you wouldn't usually buy. Read a new type of book or phone a friend you haven't spoken to in ages.

☀ **Try something creative**. It could be painting, pottery, piano or photography. Whatever it is, you'll be liberating your creative side, you'll be learning something new, you'll meet new people and you'll have fun.

☀ **Get involved in some new activity**. Maybe it's taking a dance class, joining a drama club, taking up hiking, bird-watching or a new sport. Before you roll your eyes and say you don't have the time, just give it a try. You might have to cut down on some other activity, such as TV, but you'll probably find that it's worth it.

If you feel that these things don't work for you, try to think up ones that will. But before you discount any of the suggestions, give each one at least one try. It's only when you actually try them that you will feel the impact they can have on your life.

Lighten up. Let your true spirit out of its cage and set it free to float happily.

14 Many facets to your personality

Having many facets to your personality makes you a much more interesting person.

By facets I mean the various aspects that make up the person you are. Being 'multifaceted' can make your life more exciting and can bring you greater happiness. In fact, it's possible to experience a tangible and almost immediate impact of having more facets in one's life.

The benefits of many facets

Having many facets to your personality brings many benefits, and these include:

※ Exposing you to new activities and experiences, making your life richer, more fun and exciting.
※ Introducing you to a variety of interesting people.
※ Enabling you to accumulate information on many subjects. This adds interest to your life and makes it easier to take part in stimulating discussions.
※ Making you more interesting to other people who will then seek your company.
※ Enabling you to pull yourself up into a more positive mood even if you're going through a tough patch in your life.

Each of us is different and we each have our own talents and strengths. Exploring and developing different aspects of ourselves presents us with different ways of enhancing ourselves and our happiness.

Broadening your experience of life

You might call them characteristics or interests, but whatever the label, these are aspects of yourself that can broaden your experience of life:

※ **Being outgoing and extrovert**. Even if you're shy, let yourself express a more outgoing side occasionally. We tend to feel shy because we're afraid of what others may think of us. Every now and again, perhaps when you're with people who don't already know you as shy, try to feel what it's like to be outgoing. People suddenly notice you more and you'll find yourself more included in the conversation. People are drawn to warmth and enthusiasm and it's easier to make friends in this mode.

※ **Being well read**. The more you read, the more you know and the more you can talk about. Being able to contribute to a conversation switches people's attention to you.

※ **Intellectual abilities**. Not many of us are budding Einsteins, but some focus on the intellect broadens the range of people who will welcome your presence. Knowing something about music, art, geography, politics, religions and history can draw you into new and interesting company. General knowledge comes from reading, listening and absorbing information wherever you go. Not only is it a great opener into conversation, but it brings a richness to your life.

'Having many facets makes you an interesting person'

※ **Having many interests**. Interests can span a broad range, including painting, music, collections, cooking, interior decorating, photography, wildlife, hiking, public speaking or drama. The more interests you have the more people you'll meet, the more activities you'll participate in and the more opportunities will open up for you.

※ **Being versatile and chameleon-like**. This can mean having the clothes and the poise to look stunning at a gala dinner as well as having the necessary casual gear and stamina for hiking. Happily fitting into the environment you're in brings you acceptance and friendship from others (exclude drunken parties and any kind of inappropriate behaviour from this category).

※ **Sporting prowess**. We're not all made for great sporting achievements, but this doesn't mean you can't take part in sports. If you don't try you'll never know whether you'll enjoy or even be good at something. Just being physically active brings feelings of wellbeing and is a great stress-reliever and mood-enhancer.

☀ **Being well informed about current news and events**. Staying abreast of developments, locally and internationally, makes your life more interesting and gives you even more food for discussion.

☀ **Developing aspects of your personality**. Focus on enthusiasm, compassion, taking responsibility, decision-making, leadership, ambition, welcoming change, communication skills and a sense of humour. As you develop these aspects you become more interesting and more fulfilled.

Having many sides to your personality really works. Try it, there's nothing to lose and plenty to gain!

Part Two:

Relationships, Feelings and Love

15 Relationships

'Sometimes I just want to be by myself, and I don't want to talk to anyone. Do you think this makes me a recluse who doesn't need relationships?'

The relationships in our life make our life what it is. You don't have to engage in them all the time, but without them we would be completely alone. We'd have no-one to talk to, interact, play or work with. Life would be pretty awful.

Wherever we go, we have relationships. With our parents, brothers, sisters, extended family, teachers, bosses, service providers of all kinds and many others. As we make our way through life, it's the relationships we build that ultimately have a huge impact on our happiness. Sometimes we become so busy and we forget this important fact.

The wisdom we gather about relationships is like a snowball rolling down the slope: the further it rolls, the more snow it collects. The most recent lessons remain fresh in our memory, but we also need to remember those buried deep in the snowball's core.

An ABC of good relationships

There are certain things that can do much to enhance the quality of the relationships we have. I've worked out an 'ABC' of these pointers:

Appreciation
✳ Looking for the good points in each and every relationship you have helps you realise how lucky you are.
✳ When you care for someone, show her or him. The more warmth you give, the more you'll find flowing back into your life.
✳ Good communication is the glue that holds relationships together. (For more on this have a look at Communication, Chapter 5)

☀ Everyone you know has dreams, fears and hopes of his or her own. Getting to know them and taking the time to listen moves your relationship to a new level of closeness.

Being

☀ Avoid getting involved in gossip. If you don't, sooner or later you'll be the topic.

☀ If you're angry with someone, wait till you're calm and then try to resolve the issue.

☀ Don't judge or dismiss people for simply being different to you. As long as your values don't clash, enjoy your exposure to new facets, insights, customs or attitudes.

☀ Give people the benefit of the doubt until they prove they're unworthy of it.

☀ Don't be over-sensitive and quick at presuming that someone meant to hurt you.

☀ Be honest and trustworthy, with yourself and with those around you. Say what you mean and mean what you say.

☀ If people are dishonest in small things they'll be dishonest in big ones. Avoid them.

☀ If you're having problems with a relationship, speak to someone who can help. Don't discuss your issues with the whole world.

☀ If you're experiencing only pain and unhappiness, move away from that relationship. Knowing when to walk away can save much heartache and distress in the long term.

☀ Respect yourself and others will respect you.

Connecting

☀ Nurture the relationships you care about. Give them extra time and focus.

☀ Take the time to visit sick or elderly people. You'll make a difference in their lives and it may add a new dimension to your relationships.

☀ Share a meal with friends. Even if it's a simple one, eating together brings people closer.

☀ It's the little things that make a difference. Look for little things to do to brighten someone's day.

☼ Let love be at the core of all your actions and interactions with everyone.

Relationships with your close family rate among the most important. Sometimes you may wish you could have chosen different family members, but you have to make the best of the ones you have. You need to give yourselves time – time to share, to be together and to talk. Having meals together on a regular basis is great for strengthening bonds. We lead our lives at high speed nowadays and it's easy to develop a culture of living like familiar strangers. A mealtime (away from the TV) allows us to hear each other's stories and provides an opportunity to know each other better.

If you find yourself in a difficult relationship with someone, instead of trying to change her or him try having a go at changing yourself. This may sound illogical or hard to do, but it can be very powerful. The reality is that setting out to actively change

'Relationships are the food of life'

someone else will seldom end in success. And yet, if you try a new attitude, a different approach and an alternative way of seeing things, not only do you change, but the other person changes too in response to the 'new you'. You don't have control over other people's characters, but you do have control over your own. Understanding this truth can be the most powerful tool you have to assist you with your relationship issues.

Material possessions and concerns come and go, and ultimately cannot bring deep and lasting happiness. Relationships can. Without relationships your life is empty. Having good, close relationships enables you to be the person you were meant to be. Identify the relationships in your life and see which ones could thrive better if you nurtured them more.

Relationships are the food of life. Giving them the attention they need brings you long-lasting rewards. As you go through life I hope you find love, joy and deep connection through the relationships you forge.

16 Friends

'There are one or two people I like who I see a lot of, but there are also quite a few people I like who I see only now and again. So what really is a friend?'

What is a friend?

We could probably write a whole book on this topic, but the key aspects that spring to mind about a friend are:

☀ Someone you can talk to, share things with, and argue, be yourself, cry and laugh with.
☀ Someone who sees you for what you are, your quirks, your imperfections, your vulnerability, and accepts you warts and all.
☀ Someone you can trust not to let you down, who's there for you when you need her.
☀ Someone who knows you're her true friend too and that she can rely on you.
☀ Someone you may not see for years, but when you do it's as if you were never apart.

Friends and the friendship they bring can really make our life a happy place. Without them we would be so alone. We don't even need many friends to bring happiness into our life. Just one or two can do the trick.

Different kinds of friends

Friends come in different forms, shapes, sizes and ages. You might also find that you have different friends for different circumstances. Not all your friends will fit into every situation. One friend might be a great companion in the outdoors, if hiking, camping or wildlife is your passion. Another might be a fan of music or art and will show you a world you may be unfamiliar with. Some may be gregarious and great for a good party whereas others may be shy but great to share your problems with. Just because the one may be out of place in the other's setting doesn't mean she is any less of a friend.

When you pick your friends, it's important that you pick them for the qualities you like in them and not just because they're with the in-crowd. Trying to fit in with a group that doesn't represent who you are or the values you have is not a recipe for good friendships. If you're lonely it's easier to be drawn into an unsuitable crowd because it makes you feel you belong. In the long run it's better to look for friends you identify with and to stay away from those you're not comfortable with.

Some friends come into your life for a short time and others will be with you for the rest of your life. Even those who are with you for a short while achieve some purpose. Maybe they show you something new or help you to discover a side to yourself you didn't know existed.

Every now and again you might find that someone you think of as a friend turns out not to be one. Perhaps she does things that contradict your values or tries to draw you into something that feels wrong. Friends can sometimes change and if that happens you need to make a decision. You need to decide whether you can help by intervening or whether it's best if you walk away. Your gut-feeling will usually tell you if 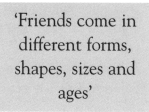 this is something serious and whether you'll be better off without this friend. I'm not talking about abandoning a friend in need, I'm talking about protecting yourself from being dragged into something unpleasant. Ending a friendship is tough, but sometimes it's the best way.

'Friends come in different forms, shapes, sizes and ages'

Close friends are very special. They are the ones you can really turn to in times of trouble, you can trust them and they won't betray you. They know you and they'll be honest with you, even if you don't want to hear what they have to say. A true friend won't hide something from you just to avoid awkwardness or becoming involved. If you have such a friend, treasure that person. True friends are not easy to find and they're hard to replace.

In today's world it can be difficult to maintain friendships because people are often on the move. They're changing cities, schools, jobs and countries.

It can be very hard when you've been close and suddenly your friends are gone. The consolation is that with communications technology, e-mail and texts it's easy to stay in touch. Nevertheless, when a good friend leaves you're left with an empty space. Other friendships will gradually fill the space, but you'll always keep a warm spot in your heart for that special person and when you see your friend again it will probably feel as if she had never been away.

Your friends can make a world of difference to your life. Let them know how much they mean to you, make time to be with them and enjoy the richness their friendship brings.

17 Different kinds of love

Love is the most beautiful emotion available to us. It is the one emotion without which we cannot thrive. Without it there is an emptiness, a hollow that cannot be filled, a yearning for the warmth only love can bring. Love is undoubtedly one of the most wonderful gifts we have. Life is another.

Three levels of love

Love can be experienced in different shades and degrees, but there are three major forms we tend to experience:

1 **Parents' love for their child.**

   This (for me) is the deepest love there is. The love we have for our own child is a love that lies ever present in our hearts. A child is a cherished gift, the most precious person to ever have entered our lives and for the rest of time will be at the centre of our thoughts, feelings and concerns.

   As the child grows up and encounters various experiences, joys and challenges, the parent is there, ready to share whatever wisdom has been learned over the years, wanting to be there in whatever way is needed. This kind of love is the most unselfish. It is one that sees parents do without so their child can have the most. It is a love that can be truly understood only once you become a parent.

2 **Love for a friend.**

   This love too can be very special. The bonds that grow from sharing common interests, values and experiences can be very strong and beautiful. The love of friendship is one to treasure. It may happen only rarely, or you may find that it comes around more often. It may last a lifetime, or it may last for a phase of your life. This love is a comfortable love. It is the secure feeling of knowing that you are there for each other, that secrets can be shared and kept, that problems can be discussed and solutions thrashed out. It is a non-judgemental emotion, one which accepts the other person for what she is and gives support as and when it is needed.

It is also a love that needs to recognise when the other person is in trouble or when she has chosen a path which is wrong. It is a love that is strong enough to support the friend and to resist your being pushed down that wrong path. The most beautiful love we can give our friends is through our presence, our caring and our conviction to be true to ourselves and the values we have.

This 'friendship' love also comes into other relationships, such as the ones you have with your parents or your partner. Friendship is something to cherish. It helps you with your whole journey through life.

3 Magical true love.

Genuine, profound love for a lover is one of the most beautiful emotions you can experience. It comes in varying degrees of intensity, but the real, deep feeling is like no other. It is a love on many different planes and it evolves as it goes along.

From the first thrill of falling in love, through the elation of having found a soulmate, to the peace and joy that loving and being loved brings – a love-filled relationship brings you untold feelings of delight and contentment. If you turn to

> 'Love is one ingredient without which we cannot thrive'

Chapter 22 on Falling in Love, particularly the section on deep and committed love, you'll find much more about how beautiful such love can ultimately be. This kind of love is truly magical, and if it ever crosses your path, treasure it, look after it – and rejoice in having the opportunity to experience such beauty.

18 Family

'You can choose your friends, but you can't choose your family.' This old saying is so true. You can't choose whom you have as family members and yet the relationships you have with them mould a large part of your life forever.

It would be wonderful if we could experience the true value of our families throughout our lives and yet, due to various situations and circumstances, we often lose sight or track of the key aspects. Sometimes, when we're young, it may be hard to fully appreciate the value of family, but as we get older those relationships grow in importance.

Why is family so important?

✵ Your first experience of emotions and events usually takes place within the family. You store many of these memories forever and they play a vital role in how you interact with others.

✵ Your family is there to share the good times with you. Even if they're not actively involved, they're still part of the infrastructure around you. If you have good relationships with them, your joy will be their joy.

✵ They're there in times of trouble. Even if you're not close, when trouble enters your life, someone in your family will be available to call upon. Friends may be available too, but they're not obliged to be there for you. Family members (unless the relationship is dysfunctional) will be there. It may mean helping you out of a mess or it may be arranging opportunities you wouldn't otherwise have had.

✵ You'll get honest feedback about yourself. No-one is quite as blunt as family. You may not like the feedback, but chances are that it'll be an honest representation of their views. I'm not referring to two-faced comments made by someone with an axe to grind, I'm talking about straight feedback about what you may be doing, wearing, planning or being.

☀ Extended family is wonderful to have. Cousins, aunts, uncles, great-aunts and even those you'd call distant cousins add a special dimension to your life. Nowadays, in many parts of the English-speaking 'developed' world, extended family is no longer given much importance. Those who do maintain close contact with non-immediate family members experience the richness this can bring to their lives.

My daughter and I recently attended a wedding within our Polish family. The small town was taken over by relations (500 of them), and the warmth, joy and love that permeated the town are hard to describe. Even meeting people I had not seen since my childhood, the intense emotion and thrill of rediscovery was so tangible it felt as if we'd never been apart.

☀ With family you have a sense of belonging. Even if you wish you had a different family, the presence of the one you have gives you that comfort of belonging somewhere. The orphaned people canvassed on this topic all express a deep longing to be part of a family.

There are probably almost as many types of families as there are families themselves, but there definitely are some specific characteristics which are identifiable. Understanding how your family interacts provides you with the opportunity of drawing the relationship closer and it brings you insight into the best ways of enhancing the elements that may be important to you.

Characteristics of families

You'll probably find that more than one of these characteristics may be present within a family at any given time. Some of them will combine to create truly special relationships, whereas other combinations will present some very challenging and difficult scenarios.

Close knit.

They know who's up to what, they do things together and they stand united when they face the world. The bonds between them are strong and there is usually a great sense of loyalty, support and helpfulness.

Loving and affectionate.

As an outsider you'll easily feel the warmth and love among these family members. You'll no doubt witness many hugs and other signs of affection, as well as being aware of empathy, compassion, genuine interest and concern for each other's wellbeing.

Cool and distant.

They may live together, but there is virtually no interaction or communication. They probably know little about each other's lives and they find it hard to express the emotion they do feel.

Many shared activities.

They do a lot of things together, often involving extended family. These activities may span a range of interests and social get-togethers, and they can even include working together.

Fight a lot.

Some families contain a mix of very different personalities or temperaments. Fighting doesn't mean that they don't love each other, it's often their way of expressing themselves. If the fights are frequent or if they become destructive, then the fabric of the family starts to be affected and an emptiness and distance can gradually settle in.

Good communicators.

You'll find many interesting and vibrant discussions taking place here. They'll tend to know each other's needs and feelings and you may hear heated debates about topical issues. The communication styles may vary greatly and can range from gentle, calm dialogue through to highly emotional and impassioned exchanges of opinion. Whichever style you encounter, the common factor will be open and flowing channels of communication that will greatly contribute towards closeness and harmony.

Mean or dysfunctional.

It's sad to see, but unfortunately there are many of these. It's hard if you're in one of these because you then have to rely strongly on yourself to cope and to avoid being sucked into the prevailing state. The only sure way of coming out on top in this situation is to seek help from someone capable, compassionate and qualified to help you through the challenges you face. It's also essential, through friendships, to find some of the elements that are unavailable to you within your family. It's not your fault if you are caught up in something you can't help and you owe it to yourself to find at least some of the protection, support and warmth you need.

Problem-ridden.

Life is not always smooth and difficulties can arise. Whether it's someone's illness, psychological problems, a mishap, drama or serious trauma, when it happens it is hard for everyone in the family. Some families seem to encounter more problems than seems fair and they can be plagued for long periods of time. The closer their relationships the more support they'll be able to provide each other and the easier these times will be to survive.

In-law challenged.

Relationships with in-laws are often made fun of and sometimes they really can be tricky. Problems typically arise for reasons such as:

* Differences in background, culture or upbringing. The in-laws may disapprove of the daughter-in-law's behaviour, manners, dress sense or other aspects.
* The parents feel threatened by the daughter-in-law. They worry that she may adversely influence their son or that their relationship with him will change. If she's an uncaring or unpleasant person this can indeed happen and their fears might be realised.
* Disappointment. Parents often have a dream in which their child's life partner is clearly envisaged. If this does not come about they may nurse feelings of disappointment. This is especially hard to deal with and can be a source of much pain for the young wife. This 'not good enough' sentiment can seep through into all aspects of her life and she may find herself harshly judged in terms of cooking, home making, child rearing and many others.
* Fear of loss. A parent's biggest fear is that of losing their child. Sometimes they fear the marriage will result in a kind of loss and they panic. Instead of realising what their fear is about and welcoming their new daughter-in-law, they surrender to their fears and end up alienating the very relationship they so need.
* Lack of effort from the bride's side. It takes both parties to make a rela-tionship work. It's vital that the new member of the family makes a big effort, not only to allay her new in-law's fears, but also to demonstrate warmth and her enthusiasm about being part of this new family.

    These can be tricky issues and they require goodwill from all sides.

There are at least six parties involved: both sets of parents plus the young couple (not to mention siblings or any step-parents in the case of divorced parents). If everyone's approach consists of openness, communication and love, then virtually all unpleasantness can be avoided. With a positive approach a potentially scary experience can turn into the joy of having a new member of the family. When your time comes one day, pour as much effort into these new relationships as you can and you'll reap the rewards for years to come.

'The relationships you have with family mould a large part of your life forever'

Which of these characteristics would describe the type of family you are part of? Even if you are fortunate enough to be in a close-knit and loving family it's always worth remembering that relationships are ever-changing. In a way they're like a living entity and they need constant attention and nourishment. Chapter 15 on Relationships, covers some tips which may be useful and may help to strengthen the family bonds.

I wish you much joy and happiness as you get to know more of (and more about) your family members throughout your life. May you experience the richness and comfort that these relationships can bring.

19 Fathers

'I sometimes feel I'm closer to you than to Dad. I'm not really, it's just that he's away a lot, we talk about different things, and so he seems so different from you.'

Fathers play a different role to mothers and it is this difference that gives them their uniqueness. Fathers come in different models and styles, physically and in terms of their personality. There are those we might deem to be 'the perfect Dad' and there are those we feel could benefit from some panel-beating. No-one is perfect, we all have our flaws and we need to focus on the relationship and the love and not on flaws we perceive.

How important do you think a father's role is in the family? How would you describe what a father is all about and what you can expect from him? Give it some thought and then let's compare notes.

Characteristics of fathers

There are some specific categories fathers seem to fall into. Everything written here is based on the assumption that these are fathers who truly love their children. Sadly, exceptions do exist and there are those who lack any fatherly instinct. They create much heartache and I'm not writing about them here.

In reality, most fathers probably show elements of each category (with the exception of the 'problem' one) at different times. You will no doubt be able to come up with more categories based on your own experience. Fathers can be classified into at least seven categories:

1 **Loving and expressive**.
   The title probably says it all. This type of father is easy to get on with, loves you deeply and knows how to show it. He will be warm and communicative and you'll know where you stand. Being expressive, he'll also

easily show when he's upset or angry, something you may find discon-
certing at times. As we've discussed, 'perfect' fathers don't exist, so you'll
have to accept occasional outbursts without becoming critical. He loves
you, he shows his feelings, he wants the best for you and he has some
rare attributes. Treasure him.

2 **Non-communicative**.

Many fathers seem to fall into this category (according to their
daughters). Some of the reasons are described in the 'Facts' section later
in this chapter, and it's worth seeing if they apply. There are fathers who
are the strong, silent type and then there are the ones who are distant and
hard to get through to. The silent ones are often deep thinkers, sometimes
shy, who spend much of their time lost in their own thoughts.

The distant fathers can be harder to understand. Their distance may
come from an inability to show emotion or to get close to people. You
might find that somewhere in their own childhood they learned that way
of being and it may be the only one they know. It doesn't mean that they
love you any less, it just means that they don't always know how to show
it. It may mean that you need to reach out to your father, tell him what
you need from him and encourage him to become more available to you.
You might not be able to turn him into an expressive person, but at least
you'll be keeping communication channels open from your side. He loves
you, so show him in every way that you love him too.

3 **Extrovert and fun**.

This father expresses much of his inner child. He is full of bounce and
vibrant ideas. Depending on your nature you'll either find him exciting and
fun or embarrassing and frustrating. He's probably got boundless energy,
he'll be entertaining friends at every occasion, partying till the early hours
and he'll be coming up with novel ideas for fun times. His way of showing
you his love is through his enthusiasm and his fun approach. Embrace his
fun nature and savour experiencing a dad who enjoys his life so much.

4 **Hard working and absent**.

This can apply to many dads. If they're in a high-pressure job they're probably working long hours and they may be away a great deal. This can be hard on you and on the rest of the family. It's easy to feel that you're not that important in his life and that if he cared more he'd be home more. You might even get on with your own life to such an extent that you stop expecting your father to play a major role in it. This is a tough situation and you need to make the best of any time you do have with him.

Working under pressure and being away from home for lengthy periods is not easy on your father. He too will be missing his family and he'll be very aware of missing out on key experiences. When he is home he may be disappointed at how tired he is and he may feel guilty at being unable to take part in more activities with his family. He may even seem withdrawn and this can be due to feelings of inadequacy or even unhappiness with his situation. Try to see things from his perspective, show him your love and remember that he loves you very much indeed. In fact, his concern about taking care of the family's financial needs is what usually drives him to work so hard in the first place. Show him that he's appreciated and tell him what you feel and what you need from him.

5 Trapped by a problem.

There are some fathers who find themselves trapped by something more powerful than they are. Alcoholism and drug abuse are among these problems, but there are others. When this happens, it can be very hard to overcome and often becomes destructive for the whole family. Such problems are not something he'll easily beat on his own, so he has to be convinced that he needs help. His chances of success depend on his willingness to admit that he has a problem and that he wants help in overcoming it. If he refuses to accept the reality, there is very little anyone else can do. Life with such a person can be lonely, scary and embarrassing, and if you ever find yourself in such a position you need to look after yourself and your emotional needs as much as possible. You need to avoid being scarred by someone else's problem.

In cases where the problem is extreme or involves physical or sexual abuse, you have to bring it to the immediate attention of someone who can help you. Sexual abuse is a horrific betrayal and you need to do everything in your power to make sure that it never happens again.

6 **Strict and fierce**.

Some fathers come across like ogres. They may be impatient by nature or believe that the father's role is that of disciplinarian. They may even act tough to cover up a soft centre. This is the way many fathers were in the 'old days'. They do love you, but they have a different way of showing it. Before you declare yourself hard-done-by, try to understand why he is the way he is.

You do get the tyrants who are impossible, but my belief is that most strict fathers are actually doing what they think is right. (In many cases their intentions are right, they might just need to ease up on the fierceness.) You need to get through to a father like this and let him know how you feel and what you need from him. If you stick to your values, are trustworthy and do your best in terms of all your responsibilities, you need to let him see that. The more he sees that he can trust you to carry out what's expected of you, the more he's able to relax his fierce hold on authority. If you can't soften him, then your only way out is to accept him the way he is, work around his 'weaknesses', welcome his way of loving you and love him back.

7 **Stay at home**.

Dads stay at home for various reasons, and sometimes these reasons can greatly affect how they are as dads. If your Dad stays home and a big part of his activities involves caring for you and your siblings, he may become very involved with his family and this gives you a wonderful bonding opportunity with him.

There are also some unemployed Dads who stay home, but who show little interest in their family. Their life is often spent with their mates or in front of the TV, resulting in scant interaction with their offspring. With such a Dad, it sometimes feels as if, even though he's physically present at home, he's actually absent. And with some such Dads the aspects described under the 'Trapped by a problem' category might even apply.

The 'stay at home' Dad who is involved and available to spend time with his children brings a wonderful dimension to his children's lives. If this is your dad, talk to him, learn from him, learn about him – and enjoy your time together to the full.

It's sometimes easy to become critical of your father when you feel that he is not living up to your expectations of him. If you ever feel that you're slipping into critical mode, try to give your father the benefit of the doubt, appreciate the love he does show you and love him in return. Even if he's not your 'dream dad', he's the one you've got and he loves you. There are so many children who don't have a dad and they would give anything to have one like yours. Accept him, love him and show him how much you appreciate his presence in your life.

Some facts about dads

When it comes to understanding fathers, there are a few 'facts' that may be worth noting:

☀ Fathers are different to mothers (obvious, but we sometimes forget it). They bring a different perspective to our lives. They interact differently with us. Their games may be more physical (or intellectual). Their way of addressing our problems will differ, as will their interpretation of life. We don't want identical parents and it's this difference that makes fathers special.

☀ Men (many, not all) frequently do not have the multitasking ability that many women do. This means that when Mum is away, Dad may struggle to fit in all daily

'Fathers come in different models and styles'

tasks such as breakfast, lunch, school lifts, shopping, homework, pets, friends and his work. Chaos might reign and he may start to panic. Don't make fun of him. Be understanding and help him where you can.

☀ Many fathers have high-pressure jobs and a great deal on their minds. They're aware of the responsibilities they carry and the more responsible they are the more stressed they can become. They may not have much spare time for the things you'd like them to do. Sometimes they need reminding that there are other things in life that are important. Don't nag, just tell them their presence is missed and remind them about their importance as a family member.

✲ Fathers have varied interests and it can be worth your while to get involved wherever you can. Whether their preference is playing football, watching sport, fishing, bird watching, woodwork, music or watching TV, you can gain a great deal from taking time to join in. Even if you're not really interested, it'll give you the to opportunity to do things together, he'll enjoy the company and your relationship will grow closer.

✲ You never know how long you've got together. None of us know how long we have on this planet, so it's a pity to waste the precious time we do have. One day, when he's gone, you'll be grateful for the extra effort you made and the time you spent with your Dad.

The relationship you have with your father is key, and being as close to him as possible opens up a world of experience which you wouldn't otherwise have. Appreciate him, love him, be patient with him when he grows old – and enjoy the time you have with him.

20 understanding mothers

'I have a very up-and-down relationship with my Mum. Sometimes we get on well and then for days on end we just fight. I wish I could understand her better.'

Mother-and-daughter relationships are fairly complex and they vary according to the personalities and circumstances involved. They also change as you grow older. Many are smooth and happy whereas some become quite turbulent. Turbulence often starts when the natural separation process begins in adolescence, and it can be a tough time for all concerned. Whatever your experience, the better you understand your Mum, and the more you communicate with her, the better your relationship will be.

Mothers summarised

Mothers, as a rule, are driven by an exceptionally powerful love for the child they brought into this world. When you try to understand your Mum, there are certain aspects to her which might be worth remembering.

Of all the people on this planet, you will probably never again have someone as committed to you, or as dedicated to your safety, well-being and happiness. Your Mum is also more tolerant of you than most other people ever will be. She'll pick up your clothes, cook your food, listen to your problems, give you advice, lend you her clothes, her make-up and her car (and probably give you petrol money, too), and once you're mobile she'll watch her house get treated like a hotel.

As you grow older and more independent, your mother will probably struggle with the natural separation process that eventually takes you to womanhood. If she tended you from birth, took you to play with friends, nursed your injuries, helped with homework, taught you to cook, paint or sew, mended your broken heart and served as a faithful taxi, it can be quite tough for her to realise that you no longer need her as much. (Dads, if they've been less involved, don't love you any less, but will often be more relaxed about you growing up.)

Most mothers also thrive on good communication with their children. They want to know what's happening in your life, how you're feeling, coping and what you're involved in. If you have good news to share with her, her delight will only add to yours.

Categories of mothers

Mothers, just like fathers, come in a huge variety of different forms. They're also very human and therefore not perfect, but they try to be the best they can. They have any number of approaches and ways of being, but they do have some common characteristics, and there are a number of categories in which they could be placed:

1 **The working Mum**.

Many of today's Mums are working. They inevitably have to manage a nifty juggling-act which comes with trying their best to be a good mother, wife, homemaker and worker. Even if Dad (or someone else) helps out, it's often Mum who carries the ultimate home and childcare responsibilities.

Some mothers are 'driven achievers' – bright, good at whatever they undertake, multitasking, flashing from one project to the next, goal-focused, with a wealth of interesting experience and information. For those around them, life might be a bit of a whirlwind, and they may sometimes feel neglected. If you have such a Mum, tell her if you need more of her time, slow her down at times, and enjoy the stimulation, learning and vibrancy that she brings you.

You also get the more 'easy-going, relaxed' Mum, working either for financial reasons, or to maintain activity or stimulation, but not so career-driven. She'll quite likely still be excellent at what she does, but her priorities may be different. Life with such a Mum tends to be more peaceful and less pressured, and may allow you more quantity time with her.

Whatever their reasons for working, Mums often battle with a sense of guilt about missing out on key aspects of their child's life. They also worry about not coping with all the demands of their career and family life, and their stress levels rise.

Talk to your Mum, find out why she works, what she enjoys, what worries or stresses her, and what you can do to help her. By showing an interest you're showing support, as well as acknowledgment of her efforts and successes. And you're able to share any problems or concerns you may have. The more you understand each other the more harmonious your relationship will be.

2 Warm and loving.

This Mum is expressive, affectionate and demonstrative, loving you in an open and uninhibited way. She's easy to get on with, easy to talk to, and doesn't hide her feelings. Depending on your nature, you'll either revel in all the emotion or, if you're more reserved, you might be embarrassed by her displays of affection. Cherish her. Don't let your shyness or reserve ever block you from receiving what she so freely gives.

3 Involved and fun.

Some mothers throw themselves wholeheartedly into their kids' lives. They're interested in everything you do, come to all your sports or cultural events, cheer you on enthusiastically, and often do activities (such as biking, drawing, gym or baking) with you. They're usually good fun, extremely supportive and occasionally slightly overwhelming. Don't feel overwhelmed. Welcome their involvement, tell them if you think it's too much and agree on a happy medium, and count yourself lucky that you're so cared about.

4 Responsible and strict.

This Mum wants the best for you, even though it feels as if she sometimes imposes unreasonable boundaries. We seldom like the words 'for your own good', but we're unlikely to find too many casualties caused by responsible boundary-setting. Today, when almost anything goes, many kids grow up with a feeling of being lost or not having clear direction, values or goals. It may be frustrating to endure certain restrictions (including those that focus on good values, morals and behaviour), but they're brilliant at building self-discipline and strength of character.

If you really feel that the rules are too strict or unfair, then talk to your Mum. Hear her reasons, and see if you can convince her of your trustworthiness and ability to be responsible. If, however, you're mixing with people whose values are questionable, or if you've slipped into any undesirable behaviour, then you need to hope that the rules will remain, and that they'll give you the strength to stick to a straight path.

5 Tough and cold.

Some mothers come across as hard and unemotional. There's often a reason for this and, if you struggle with a cold Mum, you might need to invest some time and effort into trying to understand her and into thawing her out. Try your best to reassure her of your love, and to explain your need for affection and warmth. You could also try writing to her, or slipping her a book which might convey the messages more effectively. Depending on the extent of your difficulties, a good option might be to seek advice from someone who is qualified to help.

6 Highly strung or quick-tempered.

Life with a volatile mother can be quite turbulent. Check that your behaviour isn't the cause, and then try to (diplomatically) explain to her the impact her outbursts have on you. Listen carefully to what she says for insight into some of the reasons for her reactions.

Some Mums have complicated issues of their own, ones which the rest of the family may be unable to assist with. If there's nothing you can do to ease the volatility, then try to work out the best way of coping, without taking any potentially destructive action.

7 Nags and scolds.

If you feel that you're constantly being nagged or scolded, closely examine your own behaviour first. Is there something you're doing, not doing or not hearing? Are you possibly breaking rules, being irresponsible, untidy, lazy, sulky or bad-mannered? Nagging or scolding usually happens when one person feels that the other is not carrying out his or her requests. Some parents can be overcritical or have unrealistic expectations, and if this is the case it can be really tough on you. You need to try really hard to communicate your feelings and to see if it's possible to find a mutually acceptable way forward.

8 **Mother Hen**.
This Mum may be the overprotective 'worrier', or she may be justifiably concerned if you belong to the rebel or dare-devil category. Assuming that you're not a rebel, that you're old enough for the activity and that she is indeed being overprotective, you need to reassure her that it's OK for her to let go just a little. Talk to her, hear her and then prove to her that you're able to be more independent, that you're reliable, trustworthy and well able to look after yourself.

There are many other categories of Mum, but these eight cover some of the most frequently encountered. Most mothers fit into more than one category and, at various times throughout your life, your Mum might belong more to one category than another. We all grow and change, and the dynamics of relationships are ever fluid.

Turbulent times

Occasionally, things will happen which create tension and anxiety in a family, and it can be easy to get into a negative spiral. You might do something (deliberate or not) which causes a critical reaction from your Mum. She snaps at you. You snap back. She accuses you of disrespect. You shout. And the whole situation decays, because neither of you can break the spiral. You need to be aware of this process, and not react in a way that reinforces it. Try to understand what's happening and why, and look for the most constructive way forward.

Simple, but meaningful

Some simple things count a lot, and can make a big difference to your relationship:

❉ Hugs. Most mothers love to be shown tenderness and affection. Physical affection is always special, and it's a great way of reconnecting and of expressing love or even apology, without necessarily using words. So give her a hug whenever you can.

❉ Love and recognition. We all need to feel loved, mothers included. Whether you say 'I love you', write it on a note, or show her by your actions, knowing that you love and appreciate her, and that you're able to demonstrate it, will fill her with a special peace and happiness.

> 'You never know how long you've got together'

❉ Help. For many a Mum, your acts of service confirm your love for her. She's happy when you volunteer to do stuff, because Mums don't enjoy having to keep on asking. If you offer to help with dinner, bath your little sister or do the ironing, she'll really appreciate it. And if she does ask for help, it's a good idea to do it *now* and do it good-naturedly. (No matter what good intentions you may have to help her, sighing and pro-crastination just mess it up.)

❉ Discussion. If your Mum offers an insight or interpretation that doesn't agree with yours, take time to consider it. Her wisdom may well be onto something you may not have thought of, so look at it from her perspective, mull it over and add to it if you can. If you still disagree, then debate the point with her as calmly and rationally as you can.

Treasure your Mum; there's no-one quite like her. Try to occasionally put yourself in her shoes, tolerate her quirks, appreciate her efforts and whenever possible let her know how important she is to you. And also remember that she won't be with you forever, so cherish the time that you've got.

21 Grandparents

'I wish I didn't have to go with you every time we visit Grandpa. I never have anything to do there.'

There is no-one in your life like your grandparents. They have lived in another era; their memories cover aspects of history you will only ever read about. They too were your age once, facing the challenges of growing up in a changing world. They have seen the fastest changing times of any of our ancestors, from industrial developments to medical breakthroughs, from space travel and watching man land on the moon, to computers and the Internet and all the latest technology now available. Some of the older ones even used and saw the earliest version of things we now take for granted: the telephone, car, radio, TV and air travel.

They've been in love, they've married, and they've had children. They've laughed, they've cried, they have lived and some have died. Grandparents are two generations ahead of the rest of us. Two generations of lessons learnt and insight gathered. This gives them more knowledge, experience and wisdom than you and I will have for a long time to come, if ever.

And many of them are a long way from being 'old'. Having had their own children at a young age, they might still be heading for the peak of their life's quest, often with great energy, and being great fun to be with. Their enthusiasm, enjoyment of life and own growth path make them wonderful, vibrant company, and spending time with them gives you a whole new perspective on life and on who you can be.

In today's high-speed life we so often forget to take the time to appreciate those from another generation. Too often we discount them, sidelining them for being different or for their decreased agility of body or mind. Too often we forget to truly appreciate them. Yes, some of them may be unfamiliar with the latest technology or music and they might not be able to keep up with us on a physical level, but is this a reason to forget about the person inside?

The value of the older generation

We need to ask the older people around us to tell us stories from their life, and we need to truly listen. Their memories could be turned into a best-selling book. The lessons they've learned could be made into a valuable teacher's guide. The wisdom that rests within their heart should be meticu-lously extracted and recorded. How much easier our lives would be if we could absorb from them all they have lived through and learned, instead of dismissing it.

We forget that they too faced the same type of challenges as we do. Perhaps the circumstances were different, but the challenges were similar. They clearly remember their growth and development and the painful lessons they learned. And now, if we ask, they'll share with us all these things they remember. They may look older, but inside they are the same people they were when they looked young. We forget too how much they love us. They love you in a way no-one else loves you.

If you know someone whose grandparents are distanced, maybe due to family problems or neglect, try to help them to rediscover that relationship. They'll be so glad one day. Pay your grandparents the attention they deserve. Acknowledge the wisdom they have. Spare them some of your time. So often they wait for us, hoping for the chance to know more about our lives and share with us a

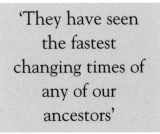

'They have seen the fastest changing times of any of our ancestors'

snippet of theirs. Our lives are so busy, there's so much to do, so many things that come ahead of visiting someone older. See past their age and into their hearts. Our busy lives won't suffer if we take a small break every now and again, a small chunk of time to show an older person that we love them, that we value their wisdom and experience, that we're grateful for their presence in our lives.

One day they'll be gone and you will have lost the opportunity forever of talking to them, learning from them, of feeling their love for you. Don't put it off. Take the time while it's there and feel the effect it has on you and your life.

22 Falling in love – and love itself

Oh what a wonderful feeling! When it happens to you it's as if the whole world changes. The colours are more vibrant, the sun shines brighter and life feels as if it's never been better. Have you felt like that yet? If you haven't yet, no doubt some time, one day, you'll feel this ecstatic joy.

There isn't anything quite like the thrill of falling in love. Sometimes it's almost instant and it hits you like a bolt of lightning. Other times it slowly creeps up on you until one day you wake up to find it glowing inside you. Whichever way it happens for you, it's still one of the best feelings there is.

is falling in love good for you?

It can be the most wonderful happening. As long as the person you've fallen for is worthy of your love and loves you back, you'll find a whole lot of good things can take place. You'll feel a surge of excitement, your positive thinking will be at its peak and you'll have a permanent smile on your face and in your heart. Your step will be bouncy, your energy levels will soar and your priorities will suddenly shift. You might also find that your brain seems to get scrambled and you're not sure whether you're thinking straight. Your appetite might even vanish and the tale of your scale might be that you're losing weight by the day. (If you do start losing weight you'll need to focus on what you're eating to make sure that you're getting the nutrition you need to stay well and strong.)

This state of being in love can be described as experiencing a natural 'high'. Whether it's hormones, enzymes or endorphins, there's definitely something that gets you buzzing from top to toe. First, there is the hot, heady, loving feeling, the infatuation and the excitement of being in love. You can think of nothing else, you miss him like crazy, you can't eat, you pine away when he's not around and you're in heaven when he's with you. You can't get enough of each other, you want to be together, hold each other, share secrets, thoughts and dreams.

When you're in love it seems as if anything is possible. You'll want to do things you've never done before. You'll miss him desperately when you're apart. All you'll be dreaming of is being with him again. When you're with him you'll feel totally complete. You'll talk about anything and everything. You'll laugh and you'll tease and your heart will leap when he enfolds you in his arms.

It's wonderful if all this happens for you with the right person, someone who will cherish your love, and who will be trustworthy and true, enabling you to feel safe in his love and in the knowledge that his intentions are pure.

Love is blind

Remember that you're at your most vulnerable when you're in love. If he's not a good person, your vulnerability can open you up to being hurt or taken advantage of. Often, when you're at the peak of your 'high', it's quite hard to see him objectively. 'Love is blind' is still an accurate saying, so even when all you can feel is euphoria, sometimes slow yourself down enough for a quick reality check.

Check with your gut-feel, your brain, your friends and even your parents, to see if it really does feel right. This is probably the time when you least want to find reasons for not being with him, but it's important that you feel good about the relationship you're going into. Even

> 'When you're in love it seems as if anything is possible'

if it feels annoying, it can be very useful to have someone who asks you the questions you may not want to ask yourself. Also make sure that you haven't totally taken leave of your senses or started to act irresponsibly.

If it feels right from all angles, then it's definitely celebration time. Time to feel all those wonderful emotions, that crazy excitement and the happiness throbbing deep in your heart. If it turns out that you've met your life's companion, enjoy building the foundations for a lifetime of deep love – if it turns out to be one of many relationships that will cross your path, then squeeze as much bliss and happiness from the time you have together as you possibly can!

When 'in love' becomes 'deep, committed love'

When you have met someone who is going to be your future partner, this is the most beautiful time of bonding, of getting to know each other, of experiencing the wonder and intimacy of another human being. Those early wild feelings slowly change into calmer and even deeper ones.

What comes next is the foundation for life. It is a process that with time becomes ever deeper, until one day you are a part of him and he a part of you. At the heart of everything that happens is communication in every form: verbal, mental, spiritual and physical. Communication is the most vital ingredient for love to flourish. It provides the golden threads that keep the relationship special forever. Those first hot feelings of love are easy, but to sustain the precious aspects is harder, so the stronger your foundation the more enduring your closeness will be.

Such profound love is rare and some people live a whole lifetime without experiencing it. Some of us may find only elements of it – and sometimes we don't know how to hold onto what we have found. It might be an experience we find only once in our lifetime, or it can visit our lives more than once. It comes with a bundle of elements all together: deep understanding, respect, passion, gentleness, sharing of thoughts, dreams and pains, companionship, friendship, compatibility, common values and beliefs – and lots of laughter and lightness of being. This love stays strong through good times and bad, and can often become stronger during times of hardship.

Other feelings can be mistaken for all-encompassing love, and yet they're not it. They may be shades of love, or perhaps infatuation, but the real love that is possible between a man and a woman is something unique.

The love I'm talking about here is completely pure. There is total respect, one for the other. There is understanding – of each other, of the feelings you experience, of the way you are and why you are. There is acceptance, a peaceful, gentle, loving acceptance of the other. We are all different, no two people will ever be exactly the same, think the same or have the same needs. Love recognises this and makes a space to accommodate the differences.

Pure love is built on complete trust. No doubts, no insecurities, no deception. There are some things that you can keep to yourself, if they're very private, have no relevance and can do no damage to the relationship in the long term. But everything else should be open to discussion. Real love knows no malice. It is gentle, supporting and places the other person first.

One day, if you ever find yourself in a position of committing to a permanent relationship and yet you feel that it doesn't contain the elements of truly powerful love, it's very important that you make your commitment happily, knowingly and with peace in your heart. The decision you make will be the right one as long as that is what your heart truly wants. Don't put yourself in a situation where you yearn for something else because this will cause turmoil, dissonance and eventual pain. It's also unfair to the one you are with, the one who loves you as best he can.

If you ever find that true and profound love, hold onto it with both hands. Don't let it go, don't forget to nurture it – and don't let the busyness of life make you forget how special this relationship is. We don't know from one minute to the next which turn our life will take. We do not know how long we have here. All the material things, our work, our belongings, the daily pressures of getting on with life, none of these are that important when compared to the beauty of love.

23 When he doesn't know you exist...

'Mum, there's this guy at school in the year above me. Every time I see him I get all awkward and flushed. I can hardly think of anything else but him, but he doesn't seem to know I exist.'

If you're infatuated and he hardly notices you, it's a very hard state to be in, but there are a couple of things you can do. Subtlety is usually your most effective option. By subtlety I mean that, instead of blatantly chasing him, you try to get him to notice you by other means. Even in the 21st century it's often far more effective for the guy to be the pursuer. It doesn't mean you don't try your best to attract him, it just means that you go about it in a more subtle way.

Should you chase him?

Don't chase him because more often than not he won't respect you for it. Ask yourself what outcome you ultimately want. Do you want to attract his attention briefly and let him see you as a bit of fun, someone he can easily have? Or do you want to kindle a real interest within him to get to know you? The second option will give you results which are different and far more satisfying in the longer term.

These days it's quite usual for girls to openly pursue guys and this is fine as long as you're aware of and happy with the outcome you might get. There are no rules here, just subtle wisdoms that have worked since the beginning of time. It's the thrill of the chase followed by eventual conquest that brings the excitement. If things come too easily they aren't as appreciated and people don't look after or hang onto them as long.

Play the game on your own terms

This boy/girl stuff is really a type of game. It's about attracting attention, making contact, feeling all sorts of wild and crazy feelings, building friendships and discovering more about yourself as you go along. What's important to be aware of is that once feelings are in the driving seat it's sometimes hard to engage the brain. Occasionally it's even hard to find the brain! So, it's better to use the brain in the early stages. Use it to help identify what you'd like to happen and ask it to help with the action plan.

Teenage boys tend to be driven quite strongly by hormones, having fun and impressing their mates. Teenage girls are driven more strongly by the heart, the excitement of romance and by what their friends think of them. (There are exceptions of course, but I'm talking about what tends to occur more often.)

Know yourself and what you're after and you'll be OK. If it's just a bit of casual fun and flirtation you want, then play the fun game, but make sure you're aware of any possible consequences. (It's also important to make sure that you're not in a situation where you are using the guy, because this is unkind.) If you're head-over-heels about someone, then approach him in a way that'll attract his interest, make him really eager to get to know you, earn his respect and let him become even keener on you than you are on him. Leave an element of mystery about you and put him in the 'pursuer' role.

When he wants to become physically more intimate, remember the hormones that drive him and that physical contact may not mean the same to him as it does to you. Only agree to things on your own terms and only once you are completely happy with everything that's happening. Also be aware of your own hormones, which do catch alight easily, and focus on keeping the brain engaged at all times! By the time you're leaving your teens, you'll be glad that you kept a firm rein on those hormones and, odd as it may sound, you'll feel more freedom and control than you would if you'd lost your reins early on. (Read the chapters on Sexuality, Sex, and Making Love For the First Time, if you're being tempted into a physical relationship.)

Walk away with pride

If you've tried everything and he still isn't interested in you, well perhaps you should accept that this relationship won't happen now and rather switch your attention to someone who will be interested. Don't get to a stage where you humiliate yourself. Walk away with your self-esteem in a healthy condition and know that if he didn't have the ability to see how special you are then he is not worthy of your attention and friendship. He's the one who lost out and you've been spared making a mistake. (A key assumption here is that you've been conducting yourself according to solid values and standards, and that he has no reason to reject you for behaving poorly.)

'Once hormones are in the driving seat it's hard to engage the brain'

Always remember the beauty that burns inside you. You are unique. You are special. You have talents. Sometimes this beauty may be buried deep inside, but it's always there, so cultivate it to its maximum potential and then don't settle for less than you deserve.

24 when you don't love him

'You know Michelle's brother, Luke? When I'm at her house we all sit around and chat and stuff, and now he says he's in love with me and wants me to go out with him. I like him, but not in the same way. I don't want to lose his friendship, but I really don't want to go out with him.'

Don't you think it's wonderful to have someone who thinks you're so special? Isn't it flattering? Doesn't it boost your confidence and your self-esteem? Maybe you should go out just once?

'Oh yuck, Mum! I'll never like him in that way!'

Gentle honesty

Sometimes you meet someone who falls in love with you and yet you don't have the same feelings for him. This can put you in quite a dilemma. It can also make you feel awkward, even guilty, that you can't seem to return the feeling. What should you do? Is there a right or a wrong way of responding?

Many of us have found out, sometimes the hard way, that being honest is so important. Be honest with yourself and then be honest with him. I'm not talking about brutal honesty, which will harshly hurt his feelings. I'm talking about being gentle, letting him down as softly as you feel is possible, but telling him truthfully about the way you feel.

Why is honesty at this time so important? Because you don't want to lead him on, making him think that you feel the same way. This raises his hopes and eventually may lead to expectations you cannot fulfil, followed by pain and even feelings of betrayal. If you care for him, you don't want to mislead him. You don't want him to feel that you took advantage of him or that you betrayed his feelings.

It's a tricky situation because sometimes you may like him a lot and being honest may mean you'll lose his friendship. Some of us have done just that.

We've hung onto someone without telling him how we feel, just so we could continue to enjoy the affection being heaped onto us. We knew we weren't playing it straight, but we were too afraid of losing his friendship. Eventually it all winds up in a complicated situation. We feel trapped, guilty, afraid and frustrated. When we do finally tell him what we feel he becomes angry, hurt and disappointed. He asks us why we hadn't told him earlier. We're uncertain of our answers. The result is that we've made his pain greater and we've put ourselves through a whole lot of turmoil which we could have avoided. Gentle truthfulness up front is ultimately better than ducking and misleading someone you care for.

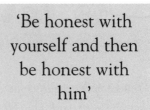

'Be honest with yourself and then be honest with him'

There are a few points worth remembering if you ever find yourself in such a situation:

☀ It is very important to be true to your feelings.
☀ There is no point in feeling guilty that you don't feel more for him. If you don't like him a lot, or if you don't love him, that's your prerogative.
☀ You're not obliged to return someone's feelings.
☀ You have a right to your feelings, but you don't have a right to use someone just to make you feel better.

Remember that old statement, 'Do to others what you would like them to do to you.' When you're in doubt about how to act, think of that statement, try to put yourself into the other person's shoes and ask yourself what you would want if the roles were reversed. Try it: it's an amazing clarifier of thought!

25 when he doesn't love you

'I think I really love Stephen, Mum, but when I told him this he said he didn't think it was going to work, and so perhaps we should split up.'

This is hard. Much harder than the other way around. You can't make someone love you and yet it's something that can be very difficult to accept.

Do you stick around or move on?

I'm assuming that you know he really doesn't love you and that you're not just jumping to conclusions. Unrequited love, loving someone who doesn't love you, is a painful experience. It's easy to say 'walk away', but it's not easy to do. You live in the hope that something will change, that he'll realise how special you are and that he'll fall in love with you and will love you as much as you love him. It also depends on the situation and how seriously you love him. A schoolgirl crush is quite normal (even when you're much older) and you'll sometimes think you're madly in love with someone only to find that it suddenly fades and your attention switches to someone else.

When you have serious feelings for him and he doesn't feel the same way, you're facing an unenviable decision. Do you stick around in the hope that his feelings will change, or do you move on? Sticking around can result in a lot of extra pain for you. It also depends on what kind of person he is. In a worst-case scenario, staying with him could end up being humiliating and destructive for you. It could damage your self-esteem, your confidence and your belief in yourself.

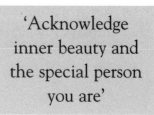

'Acknowledge inner beauty and the special person you are'

Leaving means that you lose a friendship that may feel like the most special one you've ever had. It can be a terrifying prospect and you can feel tempted to stay purely out of the fear of not finding someone better.

When you really don't know what to do, try to distance yourself from the situation and ask yourself the questions you would ask a friend if she came to you with the same dilemma. Acknowledge the inner beauty you were born with and the special person you are. Is it not true that you deserve to be loved back by the person you love? Will you ever find true, deep happiness by being with someone who doesn't really love you?

The pain of breaking away from someone who doesn't love you is great, but with time it will lessen and eventually it will fade completely. The pain of staying with him will remain with you as a constant nagging companion. You will always be faced with it, you'll be trying to understand the reasons, you'll feel the humiliation of trying ever harder to win his affection and you'll feel a sense of failure.

You deserve to have someone who loves you for the person you are. You don't have to settle for less.

26 Sexuality

Girls usually become aware of their sexuality some time in their teens. Hormones awaken the buds of sexuality within them and suddenly a whole new dimension starts to blossom within them. You suddenly become aware of the boys around you, you have crushes on some and you fall head over heels for others. Your blossoming sexuality awakens your body to feelings and sensations that are new to you. You might notice that boys frequently mature a bit later than girls do, and that's why, in your early teens, the object of your infatuation can often be a bit older than you.

Forms of sexuality

Crushes can start at a very young age, and it's not unheard of for an eight-year-old girl to be crazy about a boy, even if he's older. Sometimes crushes can even arise towards other girls. This usually has more to do with a kind of 'hero worship' than sexual attraction, and it doesn't mean that you need to question your sexual orientation.

Lesbian feelings do develop in some girls. Some are born with them, others seemingly develop these feelings in response to particular circumstances. If you strongly suspect that you have lesbian feelings then it's important to find someone whom you can confide in, someone who will give you good guidance, and someone with whom you'll be able to explore your feelings and thoughts without fear or shame. Ideally you should discuss this with your parents, but if that's not possible then pick someone who is qualified to guide you in these matters.

As your sexual awareness goes from bud to flower, you will experience for the first time the thrill of flirting, touching, kissing and arousal. The arousal you experience can be surprisingly strong and it's important that you recognise it for what it is. Arousal draws you to move from initial non-sexual touches to more intimate and sexually charged touch. Once you're aroused, touch takes on a different meaning and purpose, and can lead to the next steps of petting, foreplay and ultimately penetrative sex.

Many teens will also experience arousal and self-discovery through masturbation – a process which brings knowledge and greater understanding of your own body and reactions. Understanding your blossoming sexuality is very important in helping you to ensure that you don't get carried away and do something you'll later regret. Your hormones, once they start buzzing, can cloud your rational side, and they can lead you to experience physical intimacy at a faster pace than you would really like.

Physical intimacy, and the development of sexual relationships, is something beautiful and should not be devalued by experiencing it and experimenting with it too soon or with the wrong person. Intimacies should be shared when you're totally ready for the step you're taking and when you're fully in control of the decisions you are making. Moving forward too quickly is like putting your adolescence on fast-forward.

Don't put your life on fast-forward

The other day, I overheard a very animated conversation between two teenage girls who were planning their first kiss with a boy. There was much giggling and great excitement at what was being planned for the following Friday. After a while the realisation dawned on me that the excitement had less to do with the anticipation of a physical experience than with achieving a milestone. The one girl even admitted that she didn't know whether she liked the boy who had asked her to kiss him.

This revelation prompted me to find out more about the teenage dating scene and that in turn resulted in some interesting discussions and further revelations. It seems that my initial interpretation was a fairly accurate assessment of the reasons many teenagers take a relationship to the next level of physical experience. 'Everyone is doing it, it's expected, and if you don't do it you won't have achieved the milestone and you won't be part of the cool crowd', seems to sum up the reasoning behind the activity.

What happened to kissing someone because you are crazy about him and he about you? What happened to the anticipation, the holding back – and then 'the event'? When I asked about this, the answer was: 'It's not like that nowadays. There's no big deal to touching someone, and kissing is just one of those things you do.'

As a result of feeling so blasé and by dismissing the small intimacies of holding hands, hugging and kissing as 'no big deal', teenagers are skipping over so much. You're missing out on the whole thrill that comes when you tremble in anticipation of a touch, when your heart races and your knees go weak during a first kiss – as well as missing out on having those moments of excitement to treasure forever.

If you become blasé about the small things, you can easily become dismissive about the bigger ones too – and suddenly your life is on fast-forward. Instead of lingering over and savouring every step of each experience, you skip on in the quest for ticking off the experiences on your 'to-be-done' list.

Getting caught up in this quest is like fast-forwarding a film that has no rewind option. The more meaningless experiences you tick off on your list, the less meaning you'll find in the ones to come. And one day you'll wake up in your twenties and you'll feel a kind of emptiness and disillusion with the whole physical experience. Having raced and skipped through so much, you may feel that you're on a never-ending quest for more sensation, satisfaction and fulfilment.

So much of today's alcohol and drug abuse is about the quest for meaning and gratification. So much time, effort and money goes into seeking pleasurable experiences – and yet they are often so elusive. They're elusive because, by omitting to savour the small steps you're losing your ability to savour the big ones.

Don't put your experiences on fast-forward. Whenever you're on your way to a new physical milestone, ask yourself about your reasons for doing it. If it's just about scoring another tick on a peer-pressured list, remind yourself that life has no rewind button. Slow down, feel the meaning, let the anticipation build until you really want the experience for the right reasons – and then savour the excitement that the small events can bring.

Too fast and too far can hurt, scar or kill you

If you ever feel that you've gone too far in your physical experiences, then you need to make a staunch effort not to go there again. A strong will and self-control are essential when it comes to physical intimacy, and the more your hormones and arousal are activated the stronger your self-control needs to be.

All it takes is for you to let your control go just once and, if you're unable to apply brakes in time, you could make a mistake that will haunt you for the rest of your life. You can fall pregnant the very first time you have sex. You can also get a sexually transmitted disease (STD) or, even worse, HIV/AIDS and eventually die from your first sexual encounter.

Pregnancy and becoming HIV-positive are not small events from which you recover easily – and yet they're a very real possibility if you go too far without thinking or being prepared. When your hormones get into the driving seat, it's easy to leave your brain in neutral, and things can go wrong before you even realise that you're at risk.

Unwanted pregnancy

If you ever do make a mistake and find yourself unintentionally pregnant, it is vital that you get all the help and guidance you will need. An unwanted pregnancy is one of the most traumatic experiences you can go through, and you'll need sound advice and unwavering support from someone who cares about your predicament.

When such a shock comes your way it can throw you into a state of fear and desperation – fear about facing parents, friends and teachers, about humiliation, judgement and decisions to be taken, and fear about dealing with the consequences of the decisions that face you.

Whatever happens, don't let desperation drive you to doing something you might regret (and be unable to reverse) later. Don't let your one serious mistake drag you into making even bigger mistakes. Your life is precious and you mustn't do anything to jeopardise yourself, your safety or your wellbeing. Somehow, hopefully with someone's caring help, you need to cope with what has happened. Don't try to hide the truth from your parents or from those responsible for you, because that will only serve to make your problems worse. You need to face the reality you're in and

> 'By omitting to savour the small steps you're losing your ability to savour the big ones'

then you need to muster all your strength to make sure you take the best course of action.

Hard as life may feel at the time, the mistakes you make result in your inner growth and, as long as you remember the lessons, make you into a better person than you were before. Don't let an unwanted pregnancy break you, your spirit or the life that you've been given.

Sexuality differs for everyone

Each one of us will experience our sexuality in our own individual way. Even though the various stages of adolescent development are well known, each of us will go through them at slightly different times and in varying ways. It's a good idea to be well informed about all the various aspects and stages of sexuality so that you don't get caught by surprise or make mistakes out of ignorance. Knowledge brings peace of mind, as well as providing you with the ability to choose your behaviour and degree of self-control. Understand yourself and your sexuality, apply brakes where necessary – and celebrate what you've been given.

27 Sex and sexual relationships

Sex and sexual intimacy are the ultimate expression of love. Nothing else will bring you as close to another human being, nothing will make you quite as vulnerable, nothing will bring you the level of ecstasy the way that a satisfying sexual experience can. Mind-blowing, awesome, beautiful – there are many words that can be used to describe it.

The catch

There is, however, in my opinion, one condition that needs to be present before these sensations can be true. The sexual experience needs to take place with the right person at the right time.

There had to be a catch, didn't there? Yes, there always is when it comes to something that sounds so unbelievable. In this case though, the catch is not unpleasant. Exercising self-discipline and self-control brings many benefits, some of them unexpected, and you're most unlikely to hear anyone regretting that they waited for the 'right time'.

So what's the big deal? In today's world everyone's doing it, everyone's happy and there's no need for in-depth discussion and debate. True? Not at all. In fact, the more I seek to understand today's 'younger generation', the more obvious it is that the basic issues haven't changed. The pressures may be greater, you're exposed to a greater variety of things at an earlier age, but your basic needs are still very similar. You want to belong, to be loved, to fit in with your friends, to be attractive and desirable, to experience life – and at the same time you also want to develop your individuality. Most of all, your hormones are waking up and they sometimes feel as if they're waging war inside you. Sometimes it's hard to differentiate between your brain, your heart and your hormones. Do you ever feel like that? At times like that it can be hard to predict which of the three will win. The previous chapter on Sexuality, deals with this in much more detail.

As I said at the start, sex is quite the most wondrous and magical experience – when it's right. Have a look at Making Love For the First Time (Chapter 28), which describes how to find out whether the time and person is right for you.

The purpose of sex

When it comes to defining the purpose of sex, you can look at it in one of these three ways:

☼ As the ultimate expression of love and intimacy, between two mature adults (who are married or in a committed relationship).
☼ To have babies.
☼ As a means of having some fun and of releasing tension.

(There is unfortunately a fourth way and that's the use of sex as a tool of violence or abuse. In my opinion, anyone who does this isn't fit to be classified as human.)

My conviction is that the first two are the reasons we were given this gift, and that it's something far too special to be used as a means of recreation by people who don't care deeply for each other. Before I get shot down by the 'fun people', let's look at the reasons for my statement.

If you see sex as something that should be kept for the right time, with that really special someone, then you'll be able to experience it at its most powerful in the following ways:

☼ **You'll experience the excitement** as it builds in anticipation of the ultimate event. There's nothing that drives hormones crazier than knowing you have to wait.
☼ **You'll learn the self-control** necessary to make yourself wait for that right person and moment. Once you have it, you'll find that self-control is a liberating and empowering asset in your life.
☼ **You'll have the time to think** about what it means and about the depth of your feelings for each other.
☼ **You'll have the comfort of knowing** that you are an adult who is taking

an adult decision. You won't have to be facing the responsibilities that such a decision brings before you're ready for them.

❅ **You'll have discussed** safe sex and birth control and you'll be prepared in time.

❅ **You'll know that beautiful feeling** of being safe and allowing yourself to be vulnerable with another person. This feeling of trust and safety enables you to feel emotions you didn't know you had.

❅ **When you do make love**, all the aspects I've just mentioned combine to create that beautiful and special experience. The love-making encompasses all the expression of emotion and physical pleasure and culminates in waves of love and closeness. The more loving and committed your relationship, the greater the closeness you'll have. Making love to the man you're married to is the ultimate celebration of your union and your love for each other.

❅ **Sometimes the two of you may need time** to get used to each other's likes, desires or responses. Feeling safe within the love you share allows you to talk about this without embarrassment. Communication is important in all areas of your relationship, including the physical one. It can happen that for some reason two people are physically incompatible, but in the majority of cases it can usually be resolved with love, getting to know each other and trying other approaches.

❅ **Great love-making isn't just about a few moments** of hot passion and an orgasm. It starts long before you get into bed. Love is a great aphrodisiac and it's wonderful to delight in all aspects of your relationship. Love-making is the whole process, from a tender look to the first touch, from a first gentle kiss to wild passion and ecstasy. It's also different each time. Some times will be wild with excitement and other times may be gentle and slow. Don't set expectations, just let yourself go with the mood of the moment. Just knowing that love is at the centre of what you're doing brings you deep satisfaction and fulfilment.

❅ **Afterwards, when the fire has abated**, love remains as the bond between you. It brings you closeness and comfort and security. Love is gentle, kind and full of understanding. It is never rough or hurtful. It allows you to stay in each other's arms, in the warm safety of the bond between you.

Does it sound improbable or utopian? Maybe. And that's why it is so special and that's why it's worth waiting for. The other version of sex, the one you'd have for fun, can have great physical excitement, but it misses out on all the depth and meaning.

Sex without love

Having sex with someone you don't love and who doesn't love you may, in the very short term, feel quite good. The emphasis here is on 'short term' and on 'quite'. Following the heat of the moment, it's very likely that you'll be left with at least some of these feelings:

☼ **Emptiness.** As the passion fades, your mind and heart come back into focus. The brief physical excitement isn't sufficient to give you that glorious and lasting feeling of wholeness and love.

☼ **Doubt.** Questions come into your mind such as: 'What did that mean to him?' 'Will I see him again?' 'Am I the only one he's doing this with?'

☼ **Awkwardness.** You did all these things with each other while overwhelmed with passion, but now there are no feelings of safety and loving trust to fall back on. You can even feel quite stupid and want to get out of there as fast as possible.

☼ **Fears about how safe the sex was**. Because you're not in a loving relationship, there's no basis for trust. You don't know how many partners he's had (or has) and knowing that no protection is ever 100 percent safe you suddenly realise the danger you're exposed to. No matter what he says, if love and commitment don't govern your relationship, you're at serious risk.

☼ **It may have given you a temporary feeling** of confidence, or of being wanted and loved, but once reality returns you're left knowing that it was just a brief physical experience, and that there's nothing more to it.

☼ **Emotionally it's often much harder for the woman.** Many (but not all) women experience sex as more meaningful than many (but not all) men do. Those men are far better able to enjoy the sexual experience as just fun or a release of tension. Their needs are sometimes purely physical and they don't always attach deeper meaning to the sexual act. As an example, ask sexually active 18-year-old guys whether they're having sex for reasons of physical pleasure or of love and you'll probably find that most will say the former.

☀ **You may also experience disappointment** and a feeling that there ought to be something more and of resigning yourself to its absence. Sex is meant to be an intimate, meaningful and private experience with someone you love. If you're missing the key ingredients, you'll find disappointment in their place.

The more casual, non-loving sexual relationships you have, the less meaning you'll find in sexual contact. It's inevitable. You also won't respect yourself the way you should and neither will others. You are now seriously at risk of forever losing your ability to have that ultimate, powerful and loving sexual relationship.

Is it worth it? When you know how absolutely wonderful a mature, well-timed and loving sexual relationship can be, is there anything in this world worth losing it all for? I somehow don't think so.

Sex, at the right time, with the right person and for the right reasons, is amazing. Spoil yourself and wait for it. It's not as if you're going to miss out on something if you don't hurry. You have a whole lifetime of love-making ahead of you, so – wait for the right time and then let yourself soar!

> 'Your sexual experience needs to take place with the right person at the right time'

28 Making love for the first time

When you decide that you want to make love for the first time, it's a beautiful moment. This is your transition to womanhood – and it's a time to be savoured. If you have any doubts about whether you're ready, whether he's the right guy, whether it's the right thing to do, or if there's anything that worries you, then **don't do it.** Look at Chapter 27 on Sex and Sexual Relationships for additional important aspects.

Some important questions

Making love is something which is meant to be, and can be, so special and so beautiful. Waiting until it feels totally right is essential. If you're uncertain, then you should wait. How do you know whether it is really 'right'? Asking yourself some important questions will help you decide whether this is something you wholeheartedly want and whether the time truly is right for you:

✵ Why do you want to make love to him, now?

✵ Are you old enough for this decision? Making love is an adult experience and if you're not an adult you shouldn't be contemplating this decision. (The legal age to begin having hetrosexual sexual intercourse in the UK is 16, but even at 16 you're still not a full adult.)

✵ Do you love him? (Read Falling in Love, Chapter 22 to make sure.)

✵ Does he really love you and respect you?

✵ Are you in a committed and long-term relationship with him?

✵ Do you trust him?

✵ Will it be a celebration of love and emotion, for both of you?

✵ Do you feel under pressure to make love to him?

✵ Are you under the influence of any other factors, such as alcohol-induced passion, being caught up in the heat of the moment, or fear of any kind?

✳ Have you received professional advice and have you discussed contraception and HIV protection with him?

✳ What would you (and he) do if you fell pregnant?

✳ Is he worthy of this beautiful gift you will be sharing with him? Are you sure you won't feel any regrets about not having waited for someone more worthy of your love?

✳ Is this something you truly want, with your heart, your mind, your body and your soul?

If you feel good about **all** your answers then this could be the right time. There is no rush, no need to hurry the moment, so take all the time you need to be sure.

Make it a really special, memorable event

Once you've made the big decision, if you want to, plan the time and the place and turn it into an occasion (emotionally) for both of you. Why am I placing so much emphasis on the *right timing*? Because there's only one 'first time' and you can never turn the clock back again. When you do finally make your decision you want to remember the event as beautiful and right. Don't ever be pressured into it. If he really loves you, he'll want it to be as special as you do and he'll wait until the time is right for both of you.

Making love the first time, apart from being very exciting, can also be a bit scary. You don't know quite what to expect or how your body will react – whether there might be a bit of discomfort or pain, or just sheer ecstasy. Each one of us is different, so there's no definite prediction of what it'll be like. Read a book or two about sex, just to give you a bit more information about what to expect and what to do. Speaking to someone you can trust can also be useful, especially if it's someone who shares your values. Discussing these matters with parents can feel strange and awkward, but if you have good communication with them you could find that sharing your plans brings you an added perspective as well as unexpected advice and support.

Talking to each other about the event-to-be is also important and very helpful. It helps both of you understand each other's hopes, expectations and possible fears. Open communication is essential for a good relationship and it certainly contributes to a great love-life! If you can be open and honest with each other it deepens your love, is reassuring and dispels fears. It can be very erotic too.

Sexual experiences can vary greatly and so much depends on the depth of your relationship, your emotional connection, where you are, how much time you have and many other factors. Love-making will sometimes be so filled with emotional closeness that you'll feel like you're flying – and at other times it may be more physical. The next time will be different to the previous time and that's OK, as long as it still feels right for you. Sometimes it will be what you'd read of in a romantic novel, real Earth-moving stuff – and other times it will be quietly tender and peaceful.

> 'If you have any doubts, then don't do it'

Sometimes the first time won't be as good as you hoped and this can be for many reasons. Maybe you're too nervous, maybe he too is inexperienced, maybe you get shy. If this happens, don't let it break your heart. Just understand what happened and know that one day it can be as wonderful an experience as you've dreamed about and look forward to that day. If you really feel that something is wrong, then find out what is causing that feeling and listen to your instincts. If you don't want to do it again with this man, then don't.

I hope that your first time will be with someone who really is worthy of the special intimacy you'll be sharing with him, that his heart will be full of love, respect and tenderness, and that he will be a good and caring lover, taking care of your needs and making sure that the experience is wonderful for you – and that this will be a profound and beautiful experience for him as well.

May this be an exquisite and happy event for you.

29 Marriage

'Do you think I'll ever get married? What sort of person do you think he'll be?'

Deciding whom to marry is probably the most important decision you'll make. After that, marriage takes on a life and character of its own. The more you think about what it takes to have a happy and fulfilled marriage and the more effort you are prepared to make, the better it'll be.

What is marriage? What is its foundation? What are the ingredients necessary for a lifelong, strong, happy marriage? Some are essential, and without them there would be no starting point, but their presence alone doesn't guarantee deep fulfilment. Other important ingredients are needed for long-term survival, for real happiness, for that lasting bond and that closeness which is so different to just leading separate lives together, like familiar strangers, the way it sometimes happens.

What makes a happy marriage?

The statistics from many parts of the world state that one out of every two or three marriages ends in failure. Failure inevitably brings heartbreak to everyone involved. To avoid that heartbreak, certain key factors need to be present and need to be nourished continually. I would list the essential ingredients of a happy marriage as being:

☀ Love.
☀ Trust. Without trust there is no basis for a healthy relationship.
☀ Communication at all levels.
☀ Marrying for the right reason (and not, for example, out of fear, insecurity or for financial reasons).
☀ Common basic values.
☀ Respect for each other.

☀ Determination to resolve differences and problems as and when they arise.

☀ Being ready for the commitment and responsibilities of marriage. If you haven't completed your secondary or even further education, if you don't have at least some financial independence, or if you still want to date other guys, then it's better to wait. Confidence in yourself and your abilities, as well as a readiness to commit to one person, helps you to be more secure and at peace within yourself, and ultimately helps to maintain a balanced marriage and mutual respect. Marrying too young can place you at an unnecessary disadvantage.

There are also other factors which are important. If they're absent it's not critical, but their presence can make a big difference to your relationship, making it stronger and far more fulfilling. They are:

☀ Doing things together. Companionship builds bonds.

☀ Shared interests. This helps to find things you can do together.

☀ Your own interests which allow for individual growth and space.

☀ Give and take – being willing to understand and accommodate each other's needs and way of being.

☀ Self-assuredness and self-esteem. This avoids feelings of neediness, jealousy or clinginess.

☀ Chemistry. It's that spark that is hard to define, but you know when it's there.

☀ A fulfilling and satisfying physical relationship.

The importance of communication

After love, communication is what ensures the lasting bond, the unwavering loyalty and the commitment. It's the glue that holds the relationship steady through life's ups and downs. The communication I'm speaking of is at all the different levels: verbal, physical, mental and spiritual. You'll see that I've referred to communication in many different chapters. This is because it is one of the most vital factors in our lives.

Communication brings understanding, it brings sharing, it brings closeness. Communication is listening, hearing, absorbing and responding. At times it is also non-verbal. Only when it spans all levels is it strong enough to withstand the greatest pressures. If any level lacks strength, it brings a weakness to the whole. Such a weakness can be compensated for at other levels or with other factors, but it still leaves a weak link in the chain of marriage.

Communication – it can sound so simple, yet be so complex. The ability to share your inner self, your thoughts, fears, problems, joys, the ability to listen, to hear, to discuss, to debate, even to argue, without condemning, without contempt, without boredom, is key to communication. To listen without distraction, to truly hear, is to show respect – for your partner, his feelings, his knowledge, his opinions. Without listening there is no respect. There is a shutting off, a shutting out and eventually a shutting down. As you grow towards old age together, other activities may decline and talking to each other becomes increasingly important.

The physical part of communication is also essential. It demonstrates attraction and a need for your partner. The promise of touch, the knowledge of desire, of being the focus of that desire, that is the fertiliser that helps the garden of marriage grow. Ideally it's a feeling

> 'Deciding whom to marry is probably the most important decision you'll make'

which should be present as an undercurrent throughout the relationship and not just switched on at love-making time. Without this communication the relationship can become like a desert. It lives, but it doesn't flourish. What's interesting is that in a marriage a good sexual relationship probably counts for only about 10 per cent of the whole relationship, but if the sexual side isn't working it can count about 70 per cent. This means that if there is no physical contact or closeness the marriage could well end up in trouble.

Do opposites attract?

Sometimes it can be very exciting to be with someone who is totally different to you. It can work if you complement each other and you happily accommodate the differences. Where it gets risky is if one party starts to resent or feel threatened by the differences. The greatest risk comes if your values differ greatly. Some differences can start out looking easy to overcome, but with time they become a major problem. If, for instance, you have totally opposing moral or religious views, this can grow into something that drives you apart. Think carefully if you're aware of major and significant differences, because problems that are present before marriage invariably worsen after marriage.

Marriage is never maintenance-free

You should never take your marriage for granted, even if it seems really good. A marriage is a living entity and it never stays in one place for too long. It needs effort and attention. It's easy to see a good marriage as something comfortable and permanent and you can forget that the blossoms of marriage need regular watering to stay bright and alive.

Marriage calls for staying awake all the way through. Be sensitive to each other's needs, look at each argument from both points of view – and above all, remember that love is central to everything. Stay awake, stay in tune and experience the happiness you deserve.

Part Three:

Practical Stuff

30 Can reading be a cool pastime?

'Mum, you know I love books and sometimes I just want to be by myself and read, but my friends say I'm being boring.'

The problem is that in this age of electronic information and entertainment, reading books is not given much priority. There's so much else to do, so much fun to be had surfing the Net, watching TV and hanging out with friends – so, some people say, who needs books?

Going on a great adventure

Here's a question for your friends. Ask them, 'Can you afford not to read?' Perhaps they should answer it when they've finished reading this. I'm not saying that the Internet, TV and computer games don't have a place. Sure they do. They're fantastic, but does that mean you have to drop something equally amazing? Can reading books really be as amazing as TV and the PC? Yes and no. No – if you're reading the wrong books. Yes – if you find the right book.

So how do you know what the 'right' book is? Let me tell you a story and then you can see what you think:

In a nearby school there was a boy, his name was Sam. Sam was 16, good looking, got average grades at school, did well at sports and had a gang of friends. He had no idea what career he wanted and thought that he'd probably become a waiter, like his older brother. For entertainment he and his friends hung out in clubs and at the malls. When at home, Sam spent most of his free time playing computer games and watching TV. He scoffed at books, saying that reading was for losers and the 'older' generation. His father tried to show him the world he was dismissing,

> 'Nothing produces vibrant scenes as well as your mind can'

but this only served to irritate Sam, so he gave up.

One day Sam was riding his bike when a car hit him. Both his legs were broken and after leaving hospital he had to spend three months at home. He lay there, in pain and in boredom, half dreaming, half dozing. One day something happened that changed his life forever. He felt as if he'd been whisked away in a time machine.

By day Sam trekked across Africa with the early explorers, crossing crocodile-infested rivers, hiding from warring tribes and bartering for food supplies with local chiefs. By night he learned how to pitch camp to protect him and his men from the night's predators.

Sam got to know the ways of the Apache and the Sioux. He discovered what it takes to ride a galloping horse bareback across the plains while trying to bring down a buffalo. He found out all about plants and which ones can be used to save lives from wounds and disease.

Sam fought for his life in the jungles of Vietnam. He trained to be a good soldier and to stay alive in enemy territory. In India he learned how to protect villagers from man-eating tigers. He found out how to ride an elephant and how to train and look after it.

Sam spent a year in a concentration camp during the Second World War, watching his friends as they died of cold, starvation and bullets. He felt the anguish of the mothers as their babies were torn from their arms and he felt the cold fist of terror each time the guards looked for new 'volunteers'.

Sam ran for his life as a volcano exploded, covering the island in red-hot rivers of lava and clouds of ash. He felt his feet burn as his shoes slowly melted away. He ran until his lungs were bursting, until he plunged over the rocks into the sea.

One night Sam witnessed a gruesome murder and he recognised one of the gunmen. From then he was on the run, alone and terrified, waiting for them to catch up with him. His only hope was that the phone call he'd tried to make would alert his uncle and that someone would find him before they did.

Sam fell in love with a girl who was older than him. She taught him so much, about life and love and joy…

Sam eventually recovered, finished school and went on to become a top conservationist and pilot. His assignments take him to all corners of the world, he is married to a beautiful girl and reading is his pastime.

What happened to Sam to send him on this journey of discovery? You guessed. His father brought him books to read. One after the other, the books introduced him to new worlds, worlds of excitement, exploration, romance and adventure. Each one was different. Each one brought his imagination to life. He saw vivid scenes in his mind. He had discovered the power of the written word. Nothing can produce such vibrant scenes as well as your mind can.

Sam's story illustrates how reading will introduce you to worlds that you never imagined exist. It can make you a more interesting person and it'll give you so much more to talk about. Your brain will come alive and send you on your own journey of adventure. People will respect and admire you for your broad general knowledge. You can become an authority on topics that interest you, you'll realise that anything is possible and you'll find the building blocks for the dreams you want to fulfil. Other benefits? You can read alone, anywhere, any time. Books don't need electricity to be read (except at night), they are totally portable, they switch your brain on.

So, ask your friends again, 'Can you afford not to read? Can you afford to dismiss the world of opportunity that lies in a book?' Tell them to try it, to go to a library or a bookshop and find a book that sparks their interest. Make time to read and transport yourself into another world!

31 Your body

One thing's for sure: the body you have is the only one you'll have in your life. Some of us are very happy with what we've got and others are not so happy. At some stage in your life, the state of your body will come into focus and you will find yourself wanting to ensure that it's as good as it can be. Although looks are not everything, most of us want to look our best whenever possible.

It's a subject that has always interested me and I've explored plenty of material covering fitness, looks and health. It's certainly not possible to find all the answers, and what you read is often quite confusing because with continuous research new discoveries often contradict past ones. However, various health problems I've had along the way were a valuable lesson, combined with other concepts I've learned, and I can tell you you need to start looking after your body now!

Your health

If you're healthy you've got so much to be thankful for. It's one of those things you don't fully appreciate until you lose your health and then it suddenly takes on immense importance. It doesn't matter what you look like or how much money you have, when your health prevents you from taking part in and enjoying life, it's not much fun.

So, number one, try to do everything to make sure you're as healthy as possible. This can be boring, but it's worth it. What are the key aspects that contribute to the state of your health? What you eat is very important. The kind of lifestyle you lead, the amount of exercise you get and how you deal with emotions and problems also have an impact on your whole being. Drinking plenty of water every day is also vital because it cleanses your whole system and helps to keep your skin hydrated and healthier.

What you eat

Regular meals are important and should comprise a balanced variety of protein, grains and plenty of vegetables and fruit. The word 'regular' is important because we often forget that our bodies need a steady supply of nourishment. If you skip meals you not only deprive your body of what it needs to keep going, but you force it into storing reserves, as fat, in case you deprive it again. There is also a great deal of wisdom in the statement 'Everything in moderation'. Keeping your food varied and your helpings in moderate quantities prevents your body, and you, from feeling deprived and also stops your body from learning to expect large amounts of unsuitable foods.

There are also some foods that really don't have a good effect on you. Much as they may taste good, sweets, fast food, fatty and fried dishes do nothing positive for your health or your looks. This isn't to say you mustn't eat any at all, just keep them to a minimum.

Be Weight Wise

The best way of maintaining an ideal weight is by eating healthy foods in suitable quantities and by increasing the amount of exercise you do.

I've watched some of my friends try what seems like every diet under the sun. A particularly important lesson came from a cousin. She was not overweight, but she thought she was. She started to try various slimming products which initially caused her to look undernourished and eventually caused her whole metabolism to change. She suddenly started gaining a great deal of weight and spent the next 20 years fighting a serious weight problem. When you're young, unless you have a proven condition that requires medication, I strongly suggest you stay away from all diet products and instead turn to vegetables, fruits, fresh air and exercise.

If you are worried about weight-gain and you feel you are eating healthily and exercising regularly, then consult someone reputable who specialises in nutrition. When you choose a solution, check to see if it's natural and if it'll give you long-term results without any negative side effects.

Exercise

Exercise can be the most amazing solution to so many problems. I'm not saying you should become a marathon runner or a three-hour-a-day workout fanatic. I'm talking about regular physical activity, such as walking energetically for 20 minutes a day or playing a sport a few times a week. Not only does it make you fit, but your body becomes healthier, your weight adjusts, your face develops a healthy glow, your eyes sparkle and you have a general feeling of happiness and wellbeing. You can always tell people who exercise just by looking at them. (See Chapter 32 on Exercise for ideas on how to exercise, and for the benefits of various options.)

Your looks

You can't really change the overall shape of your body (without surgery, which I decidedly don't recommend), so you have to obtain the best results by using the means you have.

* **Accept what you have and then see what you can do to bring out the best.** This is the first step in feeling attractive. If you're going to obsess about a feature you can't help, you're likely to overlook your best features.
* **Look after the assets you have.** Strive for maximum health, eat correctly, drink plenty of water, exercise regularly, and don't smoke, drink or take drugs (all three have a very detrimental effect on your face and looks).
* **Manage your stress levels.** Life can be stressful – and excessive stress puts a different look on your face and can even affect your overall posture. Not all stress is negative, but I'm referring to the negative kind. Whether it's caused by workload, exams, classmates, relationships or other factors, you need to take action to relieve any adverse side effects of negative stress. Having friends, getting involved in hobbies, physical activity, socialising and laughing are all great ways of easing the stress you may be under.
* **Stay out of the sun.** Every time your skin burns it suffers damage and the ageing process is speeded up. It's quite sobering to see what the stunningly tanned models of 20 and 30 years ago look like today. And

not only does the sun age your skin, but it is responsible for the rapidly increasing occurrences of skin cancer and melanoma. It's not just your looks you're gambling with, it's your life. The rule is: always apply sunscreen.

☀ **Use light make-up to enhance your best features.** Subtle make-up in the form of eye-shadow, mascara, blusher, eyebrow pencil or lipstick can bring out a beauty which you, or others, may have been unaware of. The emphasis is on subtlety because heavy make-up seldom does justice and frequently results in making you look aged, haggard or plain unattractive. 'Subtle' means applying make-up in such a way that it isn't really noticeable, but your enhanced beauty sure is. (Using make-up from too young an age is not a good idea because it alters your naturally youthful beauty and replaces it with a look which, to the observer, can be unappealing and inappropriate.)

Cleanliness and personal hygiene

Looking after your body also includes a daily cleansing routine. To feel and look good you need to be clean, with clean clothes, hair and teeth. This may sound obvious, but it's surprising how many people overlook this point. Once puberty starts for girls, the focus on personal hygiene becomes more crucial than it was before. Regular showers or baths are essential and your hair needs to be washed more often. (A girl I was at college with didn't wash daily, didn't smell good, had bad breath and yet always wondered why she wasn't popular. Even a gift of soap and deodorant didn't get the message across.)

Skin care is also important in making you look good and as a means of minimising skin problems – and should include daily cleansing, moisturising and, for those in sunny climates, the recommended sunscreen.

Periods

An occurrence which arrives in puberty and sticks around till our 40s or 50s is our monthly period. Different people and different cultures have their own approach to this event and it ranges from outright dread to a joyful celebration of womanhood.

The reality is that women have periods and we need to cope with them as well as possible. When they first start they can be very erratic and their irregularity can catch you embarrassingly unaware. It's good always to be prepared, wherever you are and no matter how long since your last one.

If at all possible, it's worthwhile openly discussing periods with your mother. Not only has she had to deal with the effects you're facing, but her experience and knowledge can be most helpful.

Sometimes periods can be painful, so much so that getting on with your daily tasks becomes impossible. If this happens it's important to check with a doctor to ensure that nothing is wrong, and to get a painkiller that will help you through the worst days. Personal hygiene also becomes very critical at this time and you need to make sure that you wash yourself and change your underwear frequently.

If you're one of those women who suffer from extreme pain or tiredness during the first couple of days, the old-fashioned remedy of getting plenty of rest is still a good option. If your body is taking strain, then try not to overload it further with excessive physical activity or working hours. Do what you have to do and then have a rest. Lying down with a warm (not too hot) hot-water-bottle on your tummy, or soaking yourself in a warm bath can also be very soothing and helpful. Having said this, though, gentle exercise, such as walking, has been shown to improve the discomfort of periods.

Some of us also experience the much joked about PMS (pre-menstrual syndrome). In serious cases it can result in dramatic mood-swings, tearfulness or exhaustion, and it usually occurs a couple of days ahead of the period or right at the start. If you think you are plagued by this syndrome then seek some medical advice. Certain changes to your diet, as well as taking specific vitamins and minerals, are said to be most helpful. It's also important to be aware of your responses so that you can exercise some self-control and not make life miserable for all those around you!

Accepting yourself

Because you can't swap the body you've been given, it's important that you accept yourself. It's so easy to compare yourself with beautiful models and film stars and then feel inadequate. You'll do yourself a disservice if you spend your life unhappy because you don't look like them. You may yearn for their looks, but the chances are that they don't have your particular talents, your strengths or your personality. (It's also good to remember that without the special make-up, hair treatment and lighting, many celebrities look very ordinary.) You are beautiful, not just because of your external appearance, but because of the person you are on the inside. Your personality and your thoughts (the 'x' factor) radiate from you and can make you just as attractive or sexy as the most beautiful model.

Your clothes

What you wear can make a big difference to how you look and feel. Sometimes wearing the latest fashions can make you feel beautiful and confident. It is, however, always worth checking to see whether what you're wearing actually suits you. Some fashions are very expensive and not all are flattering for everyone. Know what styles and colours bring out the best in you and go for those. Working 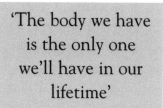 within your budget is key here, so it's often better to have a few quality items instead of numerous pieces you don't wear often.

Try on a variety of clothes when you're shopping. Seeing yourself in different styles can be great fun as well as helping to find the best ones for you. When it comes to shoes, my suggestion is to pick ones that are both attractive and comfortable. Forcing yourself into something uncomfortable can do major damage to your feet and even to your back and is not worth it in the long term. Once you've found clothes you're happy with, enjoy them and wear them with confidence and a smile!

Your personality

People are drawn to others who are positive, cheerful and caring. If you're genuinely interested in other people, if you listen to them, are trustworthy, have a ready smile and a good sense of humour, that's what will shine out from your face. When others look at you that's what they'll see and they'll want to be near you. Your appearance is only one of the elements that attracts people – personality is even more powerful.

Love and respect

It's essential to respect your body. In addition to keeping it healthy and clean, you need to treasure it for being yours. Don't let anyone abuse it. Respect your body and insist that others do the same. No-one has the right to hurt you or do things to your body that you don't want. This covers sexual experiences, violence and any unpleasant physical contact. For more information on sexual encounters, read the chapters on Sex, Sexuality and Making Love For the First Time.

... And most important of all

You've got the body you were given and, for better or for worse it's yours, so make the best of it. One day you'll be old and then your body certainly won't look as good as it does now. Don't waste time worrying about what's wrong with it, rather celebrate what's right, look after it and enjoy the life it can give you.

32 Exercise – a key to wellbeing

Exercise is a powerful, almost magical, and often forgotten solution to so many of the challenges and problems we face. Indulge in it in moderation, and see how exercise can improve the quality of your life. (I stress 'exercise in moderation' because I'm not dealing here with those individuals who go overboard and become addicted to exercise. Exercise addiction is covered in Chapter 58 When Eating and Exercise Habits Become a Disorder.) In this chapter I'm talking about the amazing improvements that exercising can bring to your life.

What can exercise do for you?

Whether you take up walking, gym, a team sport or some other physical activity, you'll soon experience the invigorating, exhilarating and liberating effects. Exercise increases your heart rate, makes your blood circulate faster, gets more oxygen to the brain and important organs, and makes your whole system function better.

The specific benefits you can experience from exercising regularly include:

※ **Improved muscle tone and definition**. Curves develop in the right places, flab is replaced by muscle, and you start to develop your optimal figure.
※ **You look good**. You can clearly see the results and, in addition to your fitter figure, your face and hair also start to glow with health.
※ **You feel good**. It's remarkable how, after you've started exercising regularly, minor ailments often disappear, your health improves and you start feeling better than ever before. You'll also find that your back is more flexible, that the backache that often comes from a sedentary lifestyle is reduced, and your increased activity eases the discomfort of periods and improves water-retention.

☼ **Your energy levels increase**. You're suddenly able to do more and you'll catch yourself going about your daily tasks with greater vigour. You might even find that you're able to enjoy longer days, with more social or other activity in the evenings.

☼ **You see life differently and your spirit feels lighter**. Exercise helps your body to release endorphins (the 'happy chemicals'), which enhance your overall state of mind. Life looks more positive, your confidence surges and you feel a greater sense of self-worth. You feel more peaceful and calm, and you'll find that you can approach challenges differently.

☼ **It does wonders for your brain power**. If you're studying or working on complex issues, the increased blood flow to the brain makes you more alert and helps your brain to be more effective and to retain information better. It also brings you fresh thoughts and new perspectives.

☼ **You have fun**. Particularly if your exercise involves other people, you'll find yourself relaxing and having fun while your fitness grows.

☼ **You'll meet people** and, if you're involved in a team sport, you'll have a sense of belonging, involvement and being part of a group. Many new friendships are made from being involved in some sporting or outdoor activity.

☼ **You'll have a sense of satisfaction** in your achievement and you might receive recognition for your efforts. You might compete and do well or even win, discovering a talent you never knew you had. A girl I know of reluctantly allowed herself to be dragged to dance classes by her friend and excelled so well that she's now winning international dance competitions.

☼ **Osteoporosis and brittle bones are kept at bay**. Exercise which involves weights and increases muscle bulk works wonders in keeping bones denser and reduces the risk of developing osteoporosis as you get older.

☼ **It's a great stress reducer**. If you're feeling stressed for whatever reason, exercise will help to wash those wound-up feelings away.

Sounds incredible, doesn't it? Well it's true – and it's available to all of us. It's available in a large variety of options, and you can choose whether you prefer to exercise alone, with a friend or as part of a team. For exercise to be effective, though, you need to do it at least three or four times a week, so decide what will work best for you.

How to choose what you're going to do

If you're uncertain about what form of exercise you'd like to get involved in, ask yourself the following questions:

1 What is your aim/goal? Do you want to get fit, be healthy, improve your looks, become competitive, or excel in a particular field?
2 Do you prefer exercising alone, with a friend or as part of a team?
3 What kind of physical activity do you enjoy the most?
4 How much time do you have on a daily basis and how many times a week would you be aiming for? If you find that you don't seem to have enough time, see whether there's something you could reschedule or do less of, such as watching TV.
5 What is your budget? Does your activity need to be free or can you pay towards it?

Have fun while you get fit

Depending on your nature, you might be a person who likes structured and disciplined fitness training programmes, or you might prefer activities which build fitness while you have fun. Here are some options you might find appealing:

☀ **Walking**. Just a 30-minute brisk walk every second day can do wonders for you. Depending on where you live, you can walk around the block or through the countryside, alone, with your dog, or with a friend. (Don't walk alone unless you're absolutely certain that it's totally safe to do so.) Walking fast uphill helps to develop great legs and calves! If there's no uphill stretch where you are, a flight of stairs can be a great substitute. In fact, taking the stairs instead of the lift whenever possible provides a good exercise opportunity. Long hikes in a beautiful setting are a wonderful way of getting fit while your spirit is uplifted by nature.

☀ **Cycling**. Riding a bike has many benefits. Among them are developing your leg and back muscles, seeing the neighbourhood or countryside, seeing a variety of gardens, and experiencing the beauty of your surroundings at a faster pace than if you were walking. (Make sure that you have safe cycle tracks, away from dangerous traffic.) If you're unable to cycle, you could use an exercise bike which you can place in front of the TV so that you can watch your favourite show while you work out.

☼ **Squash or tennis**. These sports are fun, can be competitive or social, and you don't even realise you're getting fit whilst you play.

☼ **Horse-riding**. In addition to the experience of being with such a beautiful animal, it's a marvellous way of becoming strong, toning your legs, thighs, arms and back.

> 'Life looks more positive, your confidence surges and you feel a greater sense of self-worth'

☼ **Swimming**. If you're not into training by swimming numerous lengths, you can do various aerobic exercises or play a game such as 'catch' with a friend. Swimming is a great exercise as it's non-impact and works well for anyone who has any kind of back problem or other injury.

☼ **Team sports**. Team sports can be good fun as well as bringing you a sense of camaraderie and belonging.

☼ **Jogging or running**. Running, either short or long distance, appeals to some people and not to others. If it works for you then go for it, just make sure that you avoid high-impact injuries by having the right running shoes.

☼ **Athletics, gymnastics and anything else you can think of**. If it increases your heartbeat, can be sustained for at least 30 minutes at a time, builds muscle and fitness, and it appeals to you, chances are it'll do you a great deal of good.

Tips for effective exercising

Select the form of exercise that suits you best and then discipline yourself so that you keep it up on a regular basis. It's easy to start off with great enthusiasm and then to fizzle out due to lack of motivation. Remind yourself about your reasons for exercising and set aside a schedule which you promise yourself you'll adhere to.

Avoid injury by always warming up with stretches and limbering-up exercises before you begin any strenuous exercise. If you're walking, start off slowly and gradually pick up speed.

If you're hurting, stop what you're doing. Some stiffness is inevitable during the days following the start of something new, but severe pain means that you're doing more harm than good. If you decide to take up a strenuous form of exercise, then do so under the guidance and supervision of someone qualified in that field.

Approach your chosen activity with enthusiasm – and revel in the exhilaration and sense of freedom that indulging in exercise can bring!

33 Your mind affects your health

The way you think and feel can affect your state of health. This has been proven time and again. Over the years, one of my significant learning experiences dealt with health and illness – and a most interesting lesson was about the power of emotion. Many people, if they're in good health, are unaware of this aspect and yet it is such an important one.

Your mind and your emotions definitely have an impact on how your body behaves. This does not mean that all diseases stem from the psyche, but quite a few of them can be triggered by it. Negative thoughts and painful experiences result in your body releasing 'messages' into your system which put your body into a tense state of high alert. If your body stays in this state for too long it will eventually start to destroy its immune system and can also trigger certain reactions that would normally be kept at bay. This results in disease ('dis-ease' is where the term comes from).

> 'Your mind and emotions have an impact on how your body behaves'

Factors you should avoid

☀ **Negative stress**. A certain amount of stress is healthy because it gives you purpose and motivates you to take action. Stress caused by deadlines and workload doesn't have to be negative if you can put it in perspective. Negative stress occurs when you feel you cannot cope and that you are drowning in the volume and nature of your tasks or problems. When you're constantly worrying, when you feel overwhelmed to breakpoint and when your sleep becomes disturbed, that's when you need to heed the warning bells. See what you can change and then take action.

☀ **Suppressed emotions**. If you feel angry, resentful or filled with grief, you ought to confront these feelings. You need to deal with them and then release them. If you suppress them, you're flirting with the volcano effect: for a while, all will seem fine on the surface until something blows in an unexpected place. Many people who get ill recognise that surpressing their emotions has not helped them.

✵ **Unresolved painful issues.** You might not be suppressing them, but if you continue your life dragging a heavy baggage of unresolved emotion behind you, you're heading for the danger zone. It may be guilt, anger, something from childhood or conflict in a long-lasting relationship, but whatever it is you'd do well to address and resolve these emotions.

✵ **Negative people.** Some people are just plain negative. Their glass is always half empty, their life is in a continuous mess and they complain all the time. If you try to get them to see the bright side they'll always have a reason for it being impossible. These people drain your energy if you spend too much time with them. You need your energy to fight your own battles, so when you feel it being sucked up by a negative person you should try to avoid him or her. It may not always be possible, especially if this person is a family member, but by being aware of this issue you can protect your energy supply. I'm obviously not referring here to someone who is temporarily in trouble emotionally and who needs help from you. There's a big difference between a person in need and a negative person.

✵ **Depression.** Sometimes life can throw you a hardship from which you struggle to bounce back. If you let yourself sink deeper and deeper into feelings of hopelessness you might end up suffering from depression. If this happens to you, it's important that you recognise what's happening and do something about it. Prolonged depression can have seriously adverse effects on your health. If you feel you are possibly in a depressed state, it's important to realise this is something that can be hard to beat on your own and it would be a good idea to seek help from someone who is knowledgeable in this arena.

The most important thing to remember is that your body reflects whatever you put into it. If you feed it healthy food and if you focus on remaining positive, even in times of trouble, then your chances of maintaining health are much stronger. There are many things you can do to keep yourself positive (see Chapter 5 on Attitude and 13 on Lighten Up). Do them. Not only will you be healthier, but you'll be a lot happier too!

34 Working smarter, not harder

Many people who feel they are under great pressure and find themselves working long hours, when questioned admit they are probably not working as effectively as they could. If you ever find you're drowning under your workload and that the amount of free time you have has dramatically decreased, then it may be a good idea to take a close look at your working style. (This chapter applies whether you are studying or working in a job.)

There is a big difference between just working hard and working 'smart', and in some situations as many as 80 percent of people who feel they have too much work to cope with could actually be in the category of not working as smartly as they could. There are also some people who just do not enjoy having to make an effort at all and any pressure immediately feels unacceptable to them. This discussion is not aimed at this last group – it's aimed at those who are genuinely struggling to cope with their workload.

How do you feel about your workload?

Ask yourself the following questions to help you ascertain where you are on the 'overburdened' scale:

1 Do you often feel you simply have too much to do and that there isn't enough time in which to do it?
2 Are your working hours significantly longer than before?
3 Are you often late for deadlines or appointments or find you rush at high speed to be on time?
4 Does work volume cause you to sacrifice personal relationships and make excuses to family and friends about why you aren't able to make time for them?
5 Do you always have a reason why you are the only person who can do a particular task? Do you feel overwhelmed by your workload, afraid that

you'll drown under it?

6   Has anyone who is close to you told you, on more than one occasion, that you are working too hard and that it won't do you any good in the long term?

7   Would your friends say you are often short-tempered or impatient?

8   Do you often respond to people with: 'You just don't understand how busy I am…'?

9   Do you lose things, forget about events, activities or appointments, or blame others for not helping?

10 Do you: skip meals, forget to exercise, work till late at night, get up early to work, feel stressed and anxious, and hyperventilate as you try to cope with your workload?

If you answered 'Yes' to five or more of the above questions, it would be a good idea to stop and reassess your working style to see if there's anything you could do to ease the pressure you're under. If you answered 'Yes' to eight or more, then you are in serious need of exploring ways of changing and improving your situation.

Five possible reasons for feeling overwhelmed

If your score is high, it could well be that you are currently in one of these situations:

✳ **You're a student with a non-negotiable and intensive curriculum**. The volume of work may be high, but there's always the comfort that it will all be completed in the short to medium term. How hard you work determines the grades you'll get, so focusing on the most effective methods will help you achieve your optimum performance.

✳ **You're working on a specific project**. Specific tasks or projects usually involve some form of deadline and this commonly results in periods of intense activity and extra workload, followed by a return to balance and normality. The best option is to work as effectively as you can, ask for help if you're not coping, and look forward to reaching completion.

☀ **You're under-qualified for the task**. You need a particular set of skills to perform a specific task, and if you're lacking in the skills needed you'll find yourself becoming quite stressed. If this occurs it is essential to ask for help and to work out how to obtain the appropriate skills or, if that's not possible, to then be re-assigned to a different task.

☀ **You're not being as effective as you could be**. Hard as it may be to accept, there's a very good chance that you're not 'working smart'. As I mentioned earlier, a large percentage of people fall into this category – and they experience stress and coping problems that could quite easily be avoided.

☀ **You're working for a company that is acutely understaffed**. Reasons for understaffing usually include financial difficulties, staff retention problems, or poor management. If your workload becomes intolerable and nothing can be done to reduce it, then it's probably a good idea to reassess your reasons for working there, to weigh the pros and cons, and then to consider looking for something more suitable.

What should you do to 'work smart'?

There are certain guidelines which, if you follow them, can greatly help you to work as effectively as possible:

☀ **Be honest with yourself**. Acknowledge your current working style and any weaknesses you may have – and then you need to address those weaknesses.

☀ **Be well organised**. Draw up a 'to do' list which reflects all the tasks you have to do, their deadlines, their priority ratings and the estimated time needed.

☀ **Be self-disciplined and able to say 'no'**. Tackle all the important items, resist doing the more interesting or easier ones first, and have the strength to refuse additional distracting or unimportant requests, unless they are relevant.

☀ **Manage time well**. Learn to estimate accurately the time you require for your various activities, schedule appointments/meetings at appropriate intervals (and then don't overrun the allocated time), anticipate and allow for unexpected requests, and be disciplined. It helps to remind yourself that anyone can be a good time manager if they so desire.

※ **Take regular breaks**. Breaks and daily exercise are essential to smart functioning. When you get caught up in stress and pressure it's easy to find every excuse for not exercising or taking time off. The excuses eventually backfire because you might think you're working at peak effectiveness, but you're not. Breaks and exercise clear the mind, bring more oxygen into your system and provide you with a fresh perspective.

※ **Take a bird's-eye view of your workload**. This helps you keep a check on your 'smartness' factor, assess your behaviour and performance, and prevents you from falling back into ineffective comfort zones and habits.

※ **Remember the 80-20 rule in the working environment**. It has been established that in many instances 80 percent of results come from 20 percent of the activity. This obviously varies according to profession. It's worth checking whether this could be true in your specific situation and if it is, to identify the key 20 percent and then to put a big percentage of your effort into it.

※ **Convey your concerns to someone in authority**. If you strongly feel you are indeed unfairly overloaded or underqualified for the task, it is important to raise this concern with someone who is in a position to help reduce the workload. It is, however, important to do this correctly. You need to ensure that you come across credibly, have all the facts outlined objectively, and communicate them calmly and constructively.

It's also important to remember that in virtually every study or working environment there will inevitably be high-stress and peak-activity times at some stage, so avoid being too quick to declare yourself overloaded. Usually these stages are fairly short-lived, but certain factors can make them last longer and you then need to ensure that you cope as best you can. Some level of stress is also necessary as it helps to keep your performance and productivity up. (The saying, 'If you want something done urgently, give it to a busy person', is very true, because a busy person has to manage time well in order to handle everything.)

> 'Life is too short to be wasted on working ineffectively'

Whenever you find yourself operating in true overload mode, it's worth reminding yourself of the benefits of working 'smart' versus just working harder and harder. Surely life is too short to be wasted on working ineffectively?

35 being a leader

You might want to be in a leadership role or you might dread it. You might be a natural, 'born' leader or you may need to work hard at acquiring the skills you need. Chances are that some time, somewhere, you will find yourself in a leadership position.

Situations which may require leadership skills arise in almost all walks of life: at school, on the sports field, in group projects, clubs, committees, and in most working scenarios. Although this chapter addresses leadership skills, you may not be cut out to be a leader and you then have to recognise the importance of being a second-in-command or team member, and you need to throw yourself wholeheartedly into the role you are given.

Attributes you need

If you are not born as a natural leader, suddenly finding yourself in a position that requires you to lead can be quite daunting. This subject has always fascinated me and over the years I have made a number of observations. Here's a summary of the attributes that are common among the effective leaders I have observed:

☀ **You need to be respected by others**. Forcing your authority is never effective. People need to feel confident that you have what it takes to lead them along the best path. Remember too that respect cannot be demanded or bought, it has to be earned.

☀ **You need to be competent**. This doesn't mean you always have to be an expert in all aspects of the task, but you need a good grasp of what's required. You need to understand what's involved, the decisions to be made and the actions to be taken.

☀ **You need to have vision**. You must be able to see the 'big picture' and then to draw up a plan of how it can be achieved. You're the one who shows the picture of the destination, sketches a map of how to get there and inspires those who will then build the road to the place.

☀ **Your people skills should be well developed.** Your ability to deal with people will help you in all aspects of your life. Being able to communicate effectively, earn people's trust, have empathy and be intuitive to others' needs, will make your assignment much easier.

☀ **You ought to be a good judge of people.** A large part of being a good leader means knowing how to pick the right people for the right jobs. You can't do everything yourself, so you need to surround yourself with people you can rely on to do each task well.

☀ **You must have courage.** Leading is not for the faint-hearted. You'll often have to turn your back on the crowd and venture into uncharted territory. You may find yourself alone at decision-making time and you

> 'A dose of charisma goes a long way'

might understand why it can be 'lonely at the top'. You'll also need guts when you're implementing a new idea or method in the face of opposition.

☀ **Be ethical and keep your word.** When others know that you mean what you say and that you won't let them down, their confidence in you grows. Having confidence in their leader inspires people to do their best. As a leader, it's also important to remember that you set the standards. When competitors play dirty and cut corners it can be tempting to do likewise. Playing it straight, with honesty and ethics as your motto, is ultimately the only way to long-term success.

☀ **Strive for a spirit of excellence.** Excellence in the work produced builds a sense of pride and achievement in the team. Excellence builds reputations and results in recommendations. When you're known as a leader who delivers excellence, you'll be in great demand.

☀ **A dose of charisma goes a long way.** Some people are born with it, but if you want to you can develop some of the characteristics. Charismatic people ooze confidence, enthusiasm and great ideas. The way they communicate their ideas ignites a flame of excitement in their audience. They have a great knack for understanding what others need. They're not afraid of being different and they take calculated risks. People will follow a charismatic leader even if they're not sure why they're doing it. (This can lead to trouble if the leader is misguided, as seen with Adolf Hitler.) Charisma is very powerful. Develop some of your own and watch how it can change your life.

There are volumes written on the subject of leadership and if you find that you really need those skills then it's definitely worth reading one of the simpler books. Being a leader can be great fun. It allows you to be creative, gives you freedom and responsibility, provides you with a challenge and it's never boring. Enjoy the opportunity if it comes your way!

36 Money matters

'Mum, you know I'm not great at maths, I'm never going to be an accountant, so why should I try to understand money?'

It's always good to understand the basics about money. Being confused can lead to making mistakes and those can be expensive. In my mother's day, finances were usually left up to the husband, and when he died the woman was left ignorant and vulnerable.

Even today, when women without any financial savvy end up alone they can inadvertently wind up penniless. Financial knowledge (and independence) gives you confidence, greater power and places you on a more equal footing in your relationships (both personal and work-related).

15 useful tips

☀ **Borrowing money is not a good idea.** You never know whether you'll be able to pay it back and it places you under pressure until you do. There are times when you'll have no option but to borrow, but these should be limited to important situations, such as study loans, buying a car or a house, or starting your own business (based on a sound business plan).

☀ **Don't live on credit.** It's best to live within your means and to spend only what you already have. Living on credit means that you're in constant debt and it gives the false impression that you own a lot, but in fact it all belongs to the credit company.

☀ **If you do borrow money** make sure you understand the terms:
  – When do you have to pay it back and how much interest will you be charged?
  – Put everything in writing and have it signed by the lender and by you.
  – Watch out for unethical behaviour, such as charging high interest per month: for example three per cent per month may not sound much, but

when you work it out it is exorbitant.

☀ **Understand how interest works** and how to calculate it. Don't rely on others to do it for you.

☀ **If you lend money to someone**, be prepared never to see it again. If you really need it, don't lend it. Unfortunately, the borrowing of money by friends has led to the end of many a friendship.

☀ **Pay your bills on time**. Not doing so creates enemies and costs extra.

☀ **If you can't pay your bill (or repay your loan), pay as much as you can afford** and explain the situation in writing. Pay it off as quickly as you can.

☀ **Save whenever you can**. This allows you to splash out when you really want something. If you struggle to be disciplined enough, ask whoever pays you the money to keep an amount aside for you. You obviously need to trust her or him.

☀ **Inform yourself about the best ways of investing your money**. Pick a reputable institution and select the option that suits your needs. Remember, if the returns sound too good to be true, they probably are – so stay away from that option.

☀ **Learn how to budget**. It's simple: write down how much money you get every month (income) and make a list of all the things you'll be spending it on (expenses). Subtract the expenses from the income. If your answer has a minus, cut some of the expenses. Doing this for a few months ahead tells you how much you're likely to need and how much you can save.

☀ **Jot down all your expenses** in a notebook, even if you don't have a budget. It's a record of where your money has gone and it shows you how much you need.

☀ **Make sure your mathematical skills are good enough** to protect you in all your money matters.

☀ **Don't get involved in transactions you don't understand**. Learn before you leap.

☀ As a fun exercise, when you've got time (during the holidays perhaps), come up with ideas for small businesses which could generate money for effort. Work out your cost of materials and time and see how much you'll have to sell your product or service for to make a profit. It's creative, it gets your brain working, but most of all it's a fun way of developing your skills. These are skills you will need throughout your life, no matter what you'll be doing. Who knows, this could one day turn you into a successful entrepreneur!

☀ **A little bit of understanding can be worth a lot to you.** If you're one of those people whose eyes glaze over at the mention of numbers, don't panic. Do a couple of very simple exercises just to help you to understand a little. (If you don't plant the seed you'll never grow the flower.) Giving up means handing over your power. Why open yourself to the risk

> 'A little bit of understanding can be worth a lot'

of being cheated sometime if, with a little effort, you could improve your understanding?

As a concluding thought, think about this – money is essential for us to survive and it can make our lives a great deal easier, but it is never worth sacrificing your values or your life for it.

37 To cook or not to cook?

'Why do I need to learn to cook when there are ready-prepared meals in the super-markets, and takeaways?'

Because cooking is a skill that can help you in various ways. Some people love it and some hate it. I grew up belonging to the second category, and even though I've always loved eating good food, making it was another story. It was only on leaving home that the umpteen benefits of knowing how to cook became apparent to me. And I am now passing these valuable lessons on to you.

The benefits of learning cooking basics
☀ You won't starve.
☀ It's cheaper than going out for meals.
☀ Generally, homemade food is more nutritious and contains less fat, salt, sugar and preservatives than ready-prepared dishes do.
☀ You'll impress your friends.
☀ You can invite friends over without relying on take-aways.
☀ You have friends who look forward to visiting you.
☀ It allows you to be creative.
☀ It boosts your confidence in your own abilities. Even if you're a tree-climbing, outdoor person who looks down on the domesticated species, there is a great deal of satisfaction in knowing that you can concoct something tasty.

Where to start
☀ All you initially need to do is learn to make a couple of dishes or courses. Go for easy-to-make, flop-proof, tasty dishes.
☀ Invest in a simple cookery book which contains recipes you would enjoy

– pictures are a great help.

☼ When eating something delicious at a friend's house, ask for the recipe, especially if it's quick and easy.

☼ Unless you have aspirations of becoming a cordon bleu cook, avoid all finicky recipes which require lengthy time and have zero fault tolerance.

☼ Get your mindset right: you're being creative, you're learning something and you'll enjoy the end result.

☼ When you're cooking, it helps to clean up as you go. It saves you from confronting a minefield of grease and flour at the end.

☼ Wear an apron at all times. If you don't you'll soon appreciate its value.

☼ If you're frying stuff, put newspapers on the floor to absorb the spitting fat.

'Learning to cook boosts your confidence in your own abilities'

☼ Never leave anything on the stove unattended.

☼ Enjoy what you've made. Don't be one of those cooks who get themselves into such a state during the process that they can't enjoy the results.

☼ To get you going, I'll leave you my favourite, quick, flop-proof cake (or pudding) recipe which never fails to satisfy. It takes five minutes to mix.

APPLE DELIGHT

200ml sugar	1 tin (385g) pie apples
200ml flour	2 teaspoons oil
200ml milk	2 teaspoons baking powder
1 egg	ground cinnamon

Method

Turn the oven on to 180°C. Mix all the ingredients together, except for the apples and add the baking powder last. Put the pie apples into a greased pie dish. Pour the mixture over the apples. Sprinkle lightly with cinnamon. Bake until golden brown (approximately 25 mins). Serve with cream. Enjoy!

May you have many successes in the kitchen and may your friends enjoy them too!

38 Travel

'I often dream about going to different places, but I don't know where to choose.'

If you ever get the opportunity to travel, take it. There's nothing like travel to bring completely different worlds to your door. The landscapes you'll see, the people you'll meet, the experiences you'll have – nothing else can bring you all that.

Travelling punctuates your life. Imagine if you never went anywhere. Can you remember what you did during an ordinary weekend three years ago? When you go somewhere new you'll often be able to remember the trip one day at a time. Even years later you'll be able to close your eyes and picture all the places. If you go away often, those times will be landmarks on your life's road.

When you watch the migration on the Serengeti plains, when you swim in warm, crystal blue seas teeming with multi-coloured fish, when you ride a camel through the desert, when you breathe in the air on a snow-capped mountain, that's when you know you're truly alive. When you pick berries in a

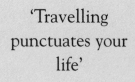

'Travelling punctuates your life'

forest, when you gaze up at the painted dome of a centuries-old church, when you breathe in the scents of a spice market, when you watch a herd of elephants frolic in a river, that's when you realise how special this world of ours is.

You can never replace the experience of actually being there. The sights, the sounds, the smells, they all remain etched on your memory forever. They expand your mind and add wisdom to your heart.

Even if you don't know how to make it happen, you can still dream and slowly work at making those dreams come true. Travel can be costly, but it doesn't have to be. Work out how much money you have and see what options this gives you. Pick the destination you find most exciting, one that will be quite different from what you already know. If your funds are limited it may mean catching a bus, sleeping in a tent and living on sandwiches, but it can be done. It may mean first exploring your own country from corner to corner, and that in itself is great. There's so much beauty waiting on our own doorstep, you don't have to travel too far to experience hidden wonders.

If you really would like to travel to foreign countries there are various ways of achieving your dream. Some options are: getting a holiday job and saving up the funds required; student exchange programmes; working visas; and foreign student organisations.

If anyone tries to dissuade you, you could list the benefits of travel for them:

☀ Travel broadens the mind. You learn and experience things you could never hope to encounter otherwise.
☀ With each trip there's a part of you that will undergo growth and change.
☀ The memories will stay with you forever.
☀ Your eyes will open more with each trip and your heart will gain wisdom.
☀ The more you see, the more you realise how much there is still to discover, to savour and to absorb.
☀ You cannot really put a monetary value on experience. (Given the choice, wouldn't you rather skip a few restaurant meals and do without a new dress than miss a romantic stroll on a tropical beach?)

As a girl it's much better to travel with a friend rather than going alone – it provides company, ensures greater safety and makes the trip more fun. Wherever you go and whatever you discover, let the experience fill your heart and your mind and your soul. Bon voyage and take plenty of photos!

39 Animals

Take the time to get to know an animal; it'll add another dimension to your life. Knowing and growing to love animals can bring a richness into your life you wouldn't otherwise have. It can touch you with a magic you'll never forget.

Pets

Having a pet animal of your own can bring a new and wonderful intensity of experience to your life. Pets make terrific companions, and they can be cute, cuddly, interesting and great fun. Before rushing out to get one, however, it's important to make sure that you're ready for the responsibility that comes with having a pet. All too often you come across a once-loved pet which is now an inconvenience, a hassle, a forgotten, discarded, neglected and sad creature.

Pets need looking after and, sometimes, after the novelty wears off, caring for them doesn't seem such fun anymore. Small caged pets such as mice, hamsters or birds need feeding, cleaning and handling, whereas dogs need far more. A dog needs affection, exercise, grooming, training and discipline. If neglected, a dog will soon look unhappy and will probably develop annoying habits, such as chewing, barking or some other mischievous, attention-seeking behaviour.

'Get to know an animal, you'll get to know a different side to yourself'

As wonderful as animals are, getting a pet means a commitment, and not just a temporary one. So you do need to be sure that either you, or someone else, will have the time, patience and finances to do the necessary care-taking. So often you hear of horror-stories in which a dog or cat is left ill or alone without food or water while the owner goes off on holiday. Such cruelty does happen and that's why, no matter how much the idea of a pet appeals, you first need to check whether you have the means of looking after it.

If making that kind of commitment is possible, or if a family member undertakes to help you, it's important to then get the right kind of pet to suit your likes and needs. You need to think about what animals (or birds) you like and look at your environment to see what kind of home you can offer. No matter how much you love a St Bernard, it won't be happy in a small apartment. Likewise, if your Dad hates loud noises, getting a raucous parrot may create serious domestic disharmony!

When you've made your decision and the pet is ensconced, it's then time to experience to the full the delight of the new relationship. You will revel in coming to know a whole new world, one filled with warmth, surprises and daily discoveries. From that moment onwards, you can just love your pet, care for it, observe and learn from it.

Let an animal touch your life

If you get to know an animal, you'll get to know a different side to yourself. Whether it's a farm animal, domesticated dog or cat or another creature, you'll find there's something special in each of them. When an animal feels safe with you, it lets you into its world. You'll see the gentleness, the playfulness and the intelligence.

Whether you're a child, a teen or an adult, animals can introduce so much into your life. Teen girls especially find companionship, affection and solace in the presence of horses, dogs, cats, rabbits and other cuddly pets. For many, specific animal breeds become a passion, with numerous posters adorning bedroom walls and ceilings, and a multitude of books being read and collected on the subject.

The spin-offs from such interests are healthy and plentiful, and include acquiring knowledge; indulging in outdoor activities; learning to care for and nurture a living creature, as well as being able to give and receive unconditional love. For many old people, and for others who live a lonely life, the presence of an animal can bring untold joy, companionship and love.

No two animals are ever the same. Even among puppies, you'll be able to see their different characters. There'll be cheeky and confident ones, clever, timid or nervous ones, brave, cowardly or intellectually challenged ones. The playfulness of animals is not unlike that of children. Even their games are similar. Kittens, for example, spend hours wrestling each other, building up strength and working out who is the toughest.

Think of all the times when animals are there for you. When you're lonely a dog will keep you company. He (or she) will love you unconditionally, will always be pleased to see you, will be thrilled to join you on a walk and will cuddle with you whenever it can. He'll nag you if you're not responding, he'll tell you when he's hungry and he'll lick away your tears when you're sad. He will protect you when there's danger, he will lead you when you're blind and he'll even rescue you when you're drowning or lost. Can you think of anything inanimate which could do all that?

The power of a horse

A horse will carry you on its back, giving you the thrill of the wind in your face and the feeling of power surging beneath. As you fly across fields and hills it's impossible to be preoccupied with life's troubles. So sleek and beautiful, with his shiny coat and rippling muscles, his alert ears, sensitive nostrils, and flowing mane and tail. A horse is the picture of perfection. As he gallops by, hooves thudding a drumbeat on the ground, neck arched and hindquarters rolling – you stop in your tracks and your heart stands still. His smell, his gentle breath on your face, his fine quivering whiskers – his eyes gentle as they gaze knowingly, reflecting a spirit deep and wise. His round shiny hooves, armed with the power to kill in one blow and yet they'll do everything to avoid trampling a human underfoot. The horse, a creature of the wide open plains, was bred for freedom and speed, to race with the wind in his mane. It takes your breath away, brings a lump to your throat and a shine to your eye. When you sit on his back, you're one with this beautiful creature and your spirit soars free…

To know them is to love them

Once you get to know them, animals can contribute greatly to your happiness – and life would feel empty without their presence. Animals bring a unique tranquillity and an awesome beauty. The better you know them the more you will love them.

Perhaps the next time you see an animal, either wild or domesticated, you'll look at it just that little bit longer and you'll feel it touch something deep inside you too.

40 Let nature's beauty energise you

Nature is a powerful healer, of stress, of pain and of sickness, in the mind, in the heart and in the body. Being close to nature brings us to the heartbeat of life and creation. To see the world that has been created for us, to experience the beauty of the wild places, is to know that we are truly alive.

Nature makes you feel alive

Nature makes life throb in our veins, it makes us come alive – if we let it. The wide open spaces, the rugged mountains, the bush and the rivers… forests, jungles, deserts, glaciers, the wind and the rain and the sun… and the solitude… in that rare silence that comes with being in the bosom of nature, that's when you feel your soul stretch out and fly.

Being close to nature can bring you a happiness that's hard to describe. Crowded cities, with bustle, grime and pollution – and politics and crime – can leave you feeling like a stranger in an unwelcome land, gasping for the breath of life. Sure, there's a place for cities, and in fact many of us will only ever live in a city – and we'll thrive on city life aspects: the cinemas, the restaurants, the shops, the buzz and the vibe. But you need the wilderness too: the desolate places, the unspoilt landscapes and the smell of grasses on the wind. It is then that your heart can truly be free and happy, even more so if you can share this with someone you love.

Our experience of the wilderness makes us realise that material possessions fade into insignificance when compared to what we've been given for free. It brings us a peace and tranquillity we could never find elsewhere.

The conservation of nature and wildlife takes on new meaning once you've had intimate contact with them. If we destroy nature – the clean air, the pure waters, the plants and the animals – our planet will cease to thrive. And yet there are so many people out there who are oblivious of this fact. They rush headlong, obsessed with the need to make more so they can throw away more, and they're blind to the truth. Even now, this very minute, we're running out of vital time to turn things around, to reverse the destruction. Conserving nature and wildlife not only assures our ability to continue seeing them, it is essential for all of us on this planet. Without nature we lose something far greater than we may be aware of.

The wilderness: a unique energiser

Experience for yourself the magical power and magnetism that takes hold of those who take the time to make nature's acquaintance. Experience how beautiful landscapes and tranquillity add to our energy of life. Even if you've never before been in the heart of nature, as you enter slowly you'll feel its spirit stir in you veins.

What is it about the wilderness that weaves this magic that entrances us? Wilderness, where wild animals once roamed free, undisturbed by civilisation. Wilderness, where you feel the pulse of nature as it throbs in the ground, the air, the vegetation and the animals, birds and other creatures.

Mere words struggle to convey accurately the mysterious allure that is unique to the wilderness, the allure that touches your spirit and your soul, the allure that draws you like a magnet and embeds itself in your heart forever, reawakening every time you're in a wild, beautiful place.

One day, when you're next to a peaceful lake or a breathtaking waterfall, walking through a rolling meadow or a scent-filled forest, or standing on a snow-covered mountain, that day you'll feel it. As you watch the crimson sun sink slowly behind the hills and you hear the night orchestras strike up, as the invisible scents touch your nostrils, you'll feel it. You'll look up at the star-filled sky above you, you'll inhale the fragrance of the wilderness and then you'll know. You'll feel the energy flowing through your veins, into your heart and into your spirit. You'll know you've never felt quite like this before. You'll wonder how you could have lived for so long without this. You'll know you'll never be the same again. You'll have felt the energy of nature…

If you haven't yet experienced these sensations, make this one of your goals in life.

Staying safe in the wilds

When you explore the beauty of nature, it's important to be aware that you're dealing with a wild and living environment, one that can vary from placid and sun-drenched to fierce and tempestuous, from rolling meadows to harsh and icy mountain crevasses, from gentle streams to frantic torrents plunging over precipitous waterfalls. Nature is beautiful, but it can be unpredictable and hazardous, so make sure you enter it in the company of a guide who knows it well. As a young woman, exploring nature on your own is definitely not a good idea. Not only do you face the natural dangers of terrain, weather and wildlife, but you could run into menacing humans who are up to no good.

> 'Being in the bosom of nature makes your soul stretch out and fly'

When you're young, the best way of experiencing nature is to do it through organised group expeditions or on summer, school or farm camps. You could also get involved with conservation or mountaineering groups, thus gaining a greater intimacy with and knowledge of the environment you're experiencing.

When you're older you can head off on journeys of discovery with other like-minded people. Always make sure that you prepare adequately for what you're planning. Going for an hour-long hike is very different to backpacking across remote mountain ranges, so the required research and equipment will vary accordingly. Inform yourself about the environment you're about to enter, evaluate any potential risks, be prepared to cope with situations which may arise – and enjoy the thrill of being close to nature.

There are so many beautiful places around the world. Places where nature paints its awe-inspiring scenes for those privileged enough to be there. Whichever one you choose to go to, don't waste another moment – don't put off that exhilarating connection for too long. Go on out, try it for yourself, soak up the experience of nature – and use it as a tonic throughout your life…

41 Music

Music is an essential part of life. We can do quite well without it, but we can do so much better with it. It can be a wonderful companion, it can reverse negative emotions and, the more aware you are of its power, the more you can use it when you need it. Music can most effectively enhance our lives.

What exactly can music do?

Once you start thinking about it, you'll no doubt come up with many uses for music which you never realised before. Some of the things music can do are:

※ **Set a specific mood.** If you want romance, tranquillity, excitement, frenzy or suspense, all you need to do is change the music.

※ **Trigger a particular emotion.** We associate music with experiences we've encountered and it can transfer you straight to a particular memory or situation as soon as you hear it.

※ **Keep you company when you're alone.** If you're alone and in need of perking up, play something lively and you'll soon feel brighter. Even just being surrounded by beautiful sound makes you feel less alone.

※ **Liberate your creative side.** Playing an appropriate piece can suddenly activate your creative juices and trigger inspiration. When you're writing something specific, such as an essay or article, playing inspiring music can do wonders to help with concepts and writing.

※ **Distract you from your problems.** If you're worrying excessively about something, putting the right music on will transport you into a different world. You might find that you'll still think about the problem, but now you'll be able to approach it differently.

※ **Provide great exercise through dance.** Dancing to energetic music on a regular basis builds fitness while you're having fun. Plus you meet people and make new friends at a dance class so, in addition to exercise, you have fun, de-stress and socialise. You can also immerse yourself totally in what you're doing, enabling you to escape for a while from life's pressures and strains.

☀ **Enhance brain power**. It's a known fact that certain types of classical music do wonders for your mathematical and learning abilities. Some people say that the opposite can also be true and that if you listen for long periods to loud, tuneless, rhythmless and harsh 'music', you can actually switch off parts of your brain. (Furthermore, very loud music can destroy your hearing, so avoid a volume that makes your ears ring or feel as if you've got cotton wool in them. Those sensations indicate damage.)

☀ **Hype you up ahead of something important**. If you've got a presentation to make or an important meeting in which you want to appear confident and outgoing, there's nothing better than listening to dramatic and energetic music on your way. I have found that the best tunes are those that start off slow and then build up to a crescendo. You can even play the piece more than once and then, by the time you arrive, you'll be

> 'Just being surrounded by beautiful sound makes you feel less alone'

buzzing all over, you'll be happy and you'll feel capable of achieving anything you want. It's quite amazing what your mind-state can do and how others react to someone who is oozing positive vibes.

☀ **Enhance emotional exploration**. Almost all forms of music can be good for setting the emotional scene for delving into and understanding yourself better. Whether it's an upbeat pop-song which cheers you up or a classical piece that calms and mellows you, you can choose the music to fit in with what you need at the time. If it feels like it's doing good then it no doubt is. If, however, your selection makes you feel heavy or depressed, then try a different one.

☀ **Influence your reactions**. Some interesting studies have been done on the effects of music on people's actions. Some shops have found that playing specific types of music can increase sales. One study showed that when you're driving a car, the louder the volume of a favourite song, the faster (and more recklessly) you're likely to drive.

☀ **Music can be used to speed up healing**. By enhancing your mood and helping you to feel positive and happier, music can actually stimulate your immune system into working harder. (Laughter has similar and even more powerful effects.)

☼ **Playing an instrument opens up a whole new world**. In addition to all the other aspects, developing an ability to play and make your own music dramatically enhances creativity, skill and even brain development. Moreover, it adds another dimension to your skills base and to the enjoyment levels you bring to yourself and to others.

☼ **Music lets you experience a type of natural 'high'**. If you're with people you like and you're ready to have fun, the right music will bring on all the positive feelings you need to have a great time. You'll find that you won't need alcohol to relax you or to put you in a party mood. All you'll need is some good music – no harmful substances, no hangovers and no other side effects, just plain music. Can you think of anything better?

Enjoy what music can do for you – it really is a kind of magic!

42 Thinking about a career

'Ever since I was a little girl, people have been asking me what I want to be when I grow up. I've wanted to be an astronaut, an artist, a writer, a marine biologist. Why doesn't one thing leap out at me?'

Choosing the kind of work you want to do is one of life's key decisions. It needs careful thought, preferably over a fairly long period of time.

Why is your decision so important?

☼ You spend more than half your waking time at work. It's important to enjoy it.

☼ It takes considerable money, time and effort to acquire the skills you need for a particular field. If you make a mistake you may not have the resources to study in another direction.

☼ If you do end up doing something you don't enjoy, it puts a damper on your whole life. If you're unhappy with your choice of career it can make itself felt in other areas of your life and you could find yourself becoming stressed, grumpy, depressed or even ill.

☼ Job satisfaction brings feelings of fulfilment, motivation, happiness and enthusiasm. When you do well, you feel a sense of achievement. Achievement results in a boost of confidence and self-esteem and this in turn can inspire you to do even better, with on-going positive spin-offs.

> 'Never underestimate the power of a good career'

☼ Never underestimate the power of a good career. It makes you financially independent, it gives you the opportunity to experience your dreams and it helps to make you a more interesting person. Even if your choice may be to dedicate yourself to raising a family, it's always worth having a skill you can rely on.

The decision-making process

When you are wondering which career to go for, there are a number of points you should consider. The more thought and investigation you undertake, the greater your chances of making a good choice.

The following steps will go a long way in helping you identify a career which will suit you:

1 **Identify where your talents lie**. What subjects and activities are you good at? What do you enjoy?

2 **Do a specific career guidance aptitude test** to see what strengths and directions that will indicate. Don't restrict yourself to its answers, rather use it as an additional tool to help you in your quest. (Being good at something doesn't always mean you'll enjoy a career in it.)

3 **See what career options are available within your field of talent and interest**. Here you need to do some research:
   – Read any relevant material you can lay your hands on.
   – Attend career expos.
   – Speak to people in as large a variety of businesses/careers as possible. Draw up a list of who you know and then ask them to introduce you to others.
   – Find out what each career option entails. Sometimes a job may sound fantastic, but in reality it may be quite different. Where possible, see if you could go along to the actual place of work so you can observe what's involved.

4 **Draw up a shortlist of the options you like.**

5 **Now find out what skills you need to have** for the various options.

6 **Find out where you'll be able to acquire the necessary skills**:
   – Ask people within those fields for their recommendations of how best to obtain the skills.
   – Contact universities, colleges and any other training institutions you feel are appropriate.
   – Obtain a description of the courses and any prerequisites you may need to have.
   – Find out how much the studies will cost and how long they will last.
   – Ask about the possibility and procedure of applying for a bursary or grant.

7 **Find out the terms and conditions** if the training is on the job. Inform yourself about the process, how long it will take, how much you may be paid at which stage and what costs you might have to bear. Also check the smallprint to see whether you're committing to work for that institution for a period after you're skilled. If so, make sure you understand all the terms. It's fair for an organisation to expect you to work for them if they've paid for your training, but you need to make sure that you're happy with the conditions.

8 **Make sure you study hard and get good marks/grades in the important subjects** if you're still at school after you've made your career decision. It can mean the difference between acceptance or rejection by the training institution you choose.

9 **Do your best.** First do your best in your studies, then do your best when you start working. The motto 'Good enough is not good enough' is a useful guideline that is worth remembering whenever you're tackling something important. In Chapter 3 on Success, you'll find some tips which have helped me throughout my career, and hopefully they'll help you too.

10 **If what you want to do seems out of reach then think again.** Before you give up the idea, explore every possible option and means of getting to where you want to be. Remember, you won't get anywhere exciting if you don't dream. Dream, then do. Never stop dreaming and never stop trying. One day you may really surprise yourself!

Some other career-related thoughts

A career is bound to have some ups and downs.
Don't expect it to always be exciting, fulfilling, fun or easy. Once you make your choice, give it a really good go. There are few careers on this planet which feel perfect from day one until the end. It's a sobering thought, but most jobs reach a stage when they can feel mundane or routine. In fact, if you look at all the jobs in the world, most are probably very unexciting. That's why education and skill-levels are so important.

Ensure that you obtain the best possible education or training.
The more you know and the better you are at doing your tasks, the more

opportunities will be available to you. If training (or education) is not available to you, then see what you can do under your own steam to learn as much as possible. If you can't afford full-time university you may have to work during the day and then study after hours. Even if it means that your socialising has to be trimmed for a while you'll find that it'll be really worth it in the end!

Your career may be different to your dream.

You may find yourself doing something quite different from what you first dreamed of, and that's OK. Life is unpredictable and you can accidentally land in something you never planned. See where it takes you and make the best of it. My dreams originally were about being a vet, but the opportunities that came up took me into the computer world. The successes that eventually came about were probably greater than any of my previous hopes and dreams, and go to illustrate the benefits of throwing yourself wholeheartedly into the opportunities you have.

There's always time for another career.

No-one says you'll have to remain in one career forever. You've always got choices. You'll always be presented with opportunities and it's what you do about them that determines your career path. An example of this could be my own experience: from a career in IT, to starting a company, to eventually selling the business, to studying photography and now to writing a book and entering a new and completely different field. Who knows what might come next? There's definite evidence that if you do your best in whatever you're doing then other new doors will open for you.

If you're unhappy, do a reassessment.

If, in spite of your best endeavours, you end up unhappy with your career, then stop and reassess everything. Do steps 1–10 on the previous pages and see what comes up. Don't be afraid. Life's too short to waste on an unhappy career.

Good luck with the process – and may your choice bring you the thrill of success and the taste of happiness!

43 Going for an interview

'Help! I have to go for an interview and I don't know what to expect, what to wear, what to say …'

At various times in life you'll find yourself going for an interview. Whether it's for a new school, a club, a job or something else, you'll stand the best chance when you are well prepared.

Preparing yourself

During the course of my career I interviewed more than a thousand people, and based upon this experience I've compiled a list of the important points to remember when you're going for an interview. Here's what you should focus on:

☼ Prepare as best you can for the interview.

☼ Find out what you can about the school/organisation. What does it do? What's its reputation like? Does it have high standards?

☼ Find out the name and position of the person who will be interviewing you.

☼ Get the address and directions on how to get there. Take a map.

☼ Put yourself in the interviewer's shoes and ask yourself what key points you would be looking for, such as academic excellence, personality, sporting ability, communication skills, experience in a field, knowledge of a topic, appearance, references.

☼ Try to anticipate the questions you may be asked and run through the answers you would give. Jot down key points for a quick revision before going into the interview. Don't take your notes in with you, unless they're brief bullet points to remind you about questions you may want to ask.

☼ Prepare questions you would like to ask. Asking a few intelligent questions shows your level of interest and tells the interviewer that you made an effort to do some homework.

☀ Remember that first impressions are *very* important. Studies have found that a large proportion of interviewers make up their minds in the first five minutes of the interview.

☀ Remind yourself of the purpose of the interview – to be accepted into a new school, to apply for a bursary, or to land a job?

☀ Dress appropriately. No matter how funky you may be it's always better to dress more conservatively. Ensure that you and your clothes are clean. Avoid any visible body piercing (other than earrings), tattoos, wildly coloured hair, very short skirts or heavy make-up. It's great to express your individuality, but an outrageous appearance seldom scores points.

☀ Run through a checklist of what you may need to bring with you: certificates, photos, project samples, ID, references, application form.

☀ Be on time. If you're early, wait outside until it's nearly time, give your appearance a final check, take a deep breath and go in.

☀ Switch off your mobile phone!

☀ Be polite to whomever you come across. Smile and be friendly. Introduce yourself and ask for the person you're there to see.

☀ If asked to wait, do so quietly. Don't chew gum, smoke, file nails or wander about. Answer when spoken to and limit your conversation.

☀ When called, stand up, smile, look the interviewer in the eye and shake hands. State your name in case he or she has forgotten it. Use a firm handshake, but avoid vice-grips and 'floppy fish'. Be friendly and follow the interviewer. Remember, first impressions are key.

☀ Sit with good posture and open body language. Don't fold your arms or lean on the interviewer's desk. If you're on a couch, sit upright and relaxed. Don't fiddle. Look at ease and regulate your breathing to calm your nerves.

☀ Listen attentively to the questions and keep your answers concise and to the point. Don't waffle. Maintain eye contact and show genuine enthusiasm. Once again, don't pour out your life story or your troubles (unless your interview is with a psychologist).

☀ Be forthcoming about your abilities and strengths, but stay modest. Bragging doesn't impress, but keeping your achievements a secret won't help either. The interviewer is unlikely to be psychic so you have to tell him or her what he or she wants to know. Show a sample of your work if it's relevant.

※ If the interviewer is experienced, the interview will probably include:
   – Obtaining information from you.
   – An opportunity for you to ask questions.
   – Some information for you about the organisation and task.
   – Conclusion: confirming the next step, timing and action to be taken.
   If the interviewer is inexperienced, he or she may stumble through without any structure. Keep calm and make sure that you still give the information needed to assess your suitability. Don't try to take control of the interview.

※ Leave the interview aware of what action is to be taken next and by whom. Confirm that the interviewer has your contact details and ask when you may expect to hear the result. Smile and thank the interviewer for his or her time.

Things not to do in an interview

There are a few definite no-nos at interview time (I have personally witnessed these and they are guaranteed to deliver an unfavourable result):

– Never put your feet on the interviewer's desk.
– Don't start to manicure your nails halfway through.
– Don't ask to use the phone so you can continue a fight with your boyfriend.
– Don't work your finger into a hole in your trousers to see how big it can get.
– Don't discuss your mother's fourth divorce and second abortion.
– Don't ask for a whisky to calm your nerves.
– Never try to make sexually suggestive comments.
– Never ask if you can sit on the interviewer's side of the desk to get a feel of what it's like to be in charge.

'A large number of interviewers make up their mind in the first five minutes'

Funny as it sounds, the people who did these things were genuinely surprised when they weren't appointed.

An interview is your opportunity to sell yourself and your abilities. Take that opportunity, prepare, believe in yourself and show that you are the best candidate!

Part Four:

Challenges & Problems

44 Your happiness: is it up to you?

'I envy my university classmates. They're always full of fun and laughter and seem to be doing so many interesting things on weekends, while I stay at home with my baby brother, my dog, the TV and my depression for company. I've never been the outgoing type, but when I look at the fun everyone else is having I so wish they would include me in their activities. I live in a large house in an expensive suburb, I dress in the latest fashions, I get good marks – and yet no-one seems interested in being my friend...'

Your happiness is in your own hands. Maybe not all of it and maybe not all the time, but mostly it is. It's quite a comforting thought, isn't it? It's good to know that you can affect your happiness and that you probably have more control over it than you realise. Here's a story you might like to think of in those times when happiness seems to be elusive:

There once was a tortoise in a lush garden full of birds and animals. As he made his slow way around, he spoke to every creature he met. Each one shared with him their problems, activities and life's dreams. He, in turn, gave them advice and a kind word. As time went by, however, he became increasingly frustrated and embarrassed by his slowness and felt that he would be much happier if he could move fast, like the other creatures. He became obsessed with this problem and one day he came up with a solution. He got himself some roller-blades.

Tortoise was ecstatic. He whizzed around the garden all day and would collapse exhausted at night. This went on day after day. As time went on, his great happiness gradually turned into loneliness and a feeling that his life was somehow empty. It finally dawned on him that by travelling at such speed he no longer had the contact with his friends that he'd had before. They didn't have the chance to share their lives with him and he didn't have their company.

Tortoise took off his roller-blades and went for a gentle amble around the garden. All the creatures crowded around him, thrilled to have him back the way they'd known him before. From that day on Tortoise alternated his days. One day he'd roller-blade and the next day he'd spend his time walking slowly around the garden, talking to all the creatures he met. When he wasn't wearing them, he kept his roller-blades on the mantelpiece to serve as a reminder of the discoveries he'd made.

His discoveries? That happiness is very much a state of mind and it's all about how we choose to see things, that sometimes travelling through life at a fast pace robs us of the little pleasures, that we sometimes don't appreciate what we have until we lose it, that having close relationships can be more important than other factors, that you can still achieve your dream without having to lose what's important. Can you think of any others?

You should try to remember Tortoise's discoveries always. Happiness is so often directly related to the way we see things. Even if you can't control the events or circumstances of your life, you can control your thoughts. The

> 'The way we think affects how we experience life'

way you think affects how you experience life. If you're unhappy, the first step you should take is to have a good look at what you yourself can do about it. There will be times when just trying to see things differently won't seem to be of help and when this happens you need to explore other ways of addressing the issues you're facing.

Sometimes there may be something very real that creates unhappiness in your life and you may indeed be a victim of circumstances. At times like these life is hard and sometimes you may have to wait for an opportunity which will allow happy feelings back into your life. In most cases, however, taking charge of your happiness can produce far more positive results than you may ever imagine.

May all these discoveries be a help and inspiration in your life and may they brighten your day every time you think of Tortoise on his roller-blades.

45 When you don't get what you want

'I am 18 now and ever since I was a toddler I've been wishing for a horse of my own. Until I was 12 we lived in a tiny house and didn't have much money. Then my Dad landed a great job and we moved to a house on a bigger piece of land, but he was travelling a great deal and still refused my request for a horse. Last year I got a weekend job so I could save up for a horse and, just as I thought it could happen, Dad's company was closed down. It now looks like we'll have to sell this house and rent something small. Life is unfair – I've been so patient and yet my wish just doesn't come true…'

Sometimes you want something so badly and yet it seems to escape you every time. If this happens, what are the options available to you? If you know it's something achievable, you can just grit your teeth and work towards it with great determination. You can work without stopping to measure the effort and without constantly being aware of how hard you're trying. You can just do your best and go all out until you can go no longer.

Is it really worth the effort?

Once you've put in a huge effort and you still haven't managed to obtain what you want, you then have to stop and check whether what you want is really worth the effort. You also need to ask yourself some questions:

✳ Why do I want this?
✳ Will getting it bring something positive into my life (and into the lives of those around me)?
✳ Can the effort do some damage somewhere?
✳ Am I sure the price is worth it?

If you're happy with the answers then you have the option of going back to trying again. Sometimes, however, what you want just does not come your way. Then what? Depending on what it was, you can put it aside to try again in the future, or you can accept that not everything you want will be granted to you.

> 'Sometimes there's a reason we don't get what we want'

To understand this is important as it helps you to move on without carrying frustration, bitterness, anger or disappointment. Sometimes there's a reason you don't get what you want and sometimes in the end it's better that way. Know that you did your best and then move on, with peace in your heart.

46 When things are tough at school

'I hate my school, and I keep asking my parents to let me go to another one, but they're refusing to do so. I've been here for seven years and everything was great until I failed last year. I'm now in a class where I have no friends, where everyone is younger than me, and where I feel that I'm being criticised for having failed. My friends from my original year don't seem to want me around as much and I just feel totally out of place. I really dread having to go to school…'

School is like a world on its own. As you enter it you're suddenly transported into that world, its activities, friendships, challenges and hardships. Sometimes school is the best experience that's ever happened to you and at other times it can be a world that you dread.

Things can suddenly turn tough for a number of reasons. Maybe the schoolwork becomes hard and you're struggling to cope. Perhaps you no longer have the friends you had before and you're filled with a heavy loneliness. You might have had a fight with someone and this has affected you more than you thought possible. Maybe you've been caught doing something wrong and you're afraid, ashamed or embarrassed.

Whatever the reason, feeling unhappy about school affects a big part of your life. It's important to try to understand the reason for your unhappiness and then to see what you can do about it. Remember, you may not be able to change the circumstances, but you can always choose how you're going to react to them.

Steps for working through the problem

Sometimes it's hard to identify what the exact problem is, so if you find yourself struggling to work it out, here's a process which can be very helpful:

✴ Write down all your feelings, good and bad.

☀ For each feeling note down what is making you feel that way.

☀ Look at the negative feelings and ask yourself if anything else could be causing them.

☀ Write down any ideas you have which could improve things for you. Let your imagination roam free, even if the ideas sound strange.

☀ Explore what you can do to change the circumstances, what someone else could do and how you can bring in more of the elements that make you feel happy. (Chapter 53, When You Need Help, might have some useful pointers too.)

☀ Now pretend that this problem has been brought to you by a friend. What would you advise your friend on each of the points?

☀ Taking all the ideas you've come up with, draw up a list of all the things you're going to do to make life easier for yourself. As you start doing them, remind yourself to check your list regularly, tick off the items when you're happy that they're working and address the ones still to be done.

If the problems are hard to solve, try to also focus on all the positive aspects in your life. At first this may be hard, but as you manage to see the good parts they can help to put your problems into better perspective for you. If you cannot change any of the circumstances around you, the only aspect you can change is how you see them.

'School is like a world on its own'

Whenever things feel really tough it's comforting to know that there's always something you yourself can do which can activate some positive change or result.

47 When you're angry

'My father walked out on us three years ago. My Mum works hard, my sister and I help around the house, and I think we've all managed pretty well. There's just one problem – my temper. I just seem to explode over the smallest thing. For example, I know that Mum does her best, but whenever I want to buy something and she says we can't afford it then my anger bursts out and I scream and shout at her – and at anyone who may be trying to calm me down. I wish I could stop these temper tantrums, but even counting to ten doesn't help…'

Anger is an emotion all of us will feel at some time or other. Expressing anger is important, because bottling it up is never a good idea. But what is also very important is to understand why you are angry and to make sure that you express your anger in the right way (smashing things or hitting someone is not the 'right' way).

As you read this I don't know what angry feelings you've felt or may even be feeling, but hopefully what you read makes some sense to you and maybe helps you through situations which may arise.

When you're young and things don't go the way you want them to, you get angry. Most of the time it's a short-lived burst of feeling, you express it and it's over as quickly as it happened. Expressing it helps you to get it out of your system.

As you get older, different things will happen around you and to you and some of these can make you feel very angry. You might get angry because someone did something to hurt you or because you couldn't have your way. You may feel that an injustice has been done or that you're helpless in some aspect of your life.

If you get angry occasionally it's a perfectly normal part of being alive. If you express it in a way that doesn't damage anything or hurt anyone then it's good. Problems start to arise if you suppress your anger. Suppressed anger and emotion is like the pressure that builds up in a volcano. For a long time you may not see anything going wrong until one day you blow up. The problem with blowing up is it usually happens without warning and on a far larger scale than was necessary. In today's world there seems to be a lot of unresolved anger which then causes all sorts of unpleasant or violent events.

When you're angry it's important to know why you are feeling like that. If you can understand the reason it's easier to make sure you express it correctly. If one person has hurt you it doesn't help to take it out on another. It's better to wait until you are thinking clearly and then to rationally work out what you think you should do. Lashing out in the heat of the moment can feel good, but you might regret it later.

You may sometimes react with anger when you feel helpless about something. Anger can be an emotion that feels safer than admitting to the real issue. If this is the kind of anger you're feeling then you need to get to the bottom of it. Perhaps you feel caught up in a situation you see no solution for. Maybe you're trapped in someone else's problems and you're feeling like a helpless victim.

Whatever the reason, as soon as you understand the real cause of your anger you can start to work out how you should react. If you don't understand, you'll be no better than a little child who flies into a rage and throws tantrums.

Some helpful pointers

The subject of anger is complex and fills volumes. I don't intend to go into a lengthy debate about it here, but instead I'd like to give you a few guidelines which can be really helpful. Here's a summary of seven points that are worth remembering:

1 Make sure you know the real reason for your anger. Sometimes it may be clear and other times you'll need to dig deep to identify it.
2 Accept that anger is not an abnormal emotion, so don't try to suppress or ignore it.
3 Wait until you're calmer before reacting, thus allowing your rational side to help you.
4 If you feel you need to explode it's best to be alone and to grab a pillow which you can pummel and scream into. Venting your anger this way is

harmless and gives you the release you need. It also spares the whole mess of venting it on someone else, doing or saying things you didn't mean, hurting them and subsequently filling yourself with guilt and regret.

5 If you're feeling angry often, it's important you make every effort to find the reason. Once you understand things better, draw up a plan of what you think you ought to do to solve the problem. It might help to ask someone's advice if you find that you're struggling to identify the reason.

6 If you realise that your anger is caused by an underlying feeling which comes from some deep and serious issue, perhaps something that happened long ago, then it's important to see someone who specialises in these sort of things. A counsellor knows the best process to follow in order to resolve feelings that may have been hidden or buried. Seeing someone is like using a map to take the shortest route home, whereas struggling by yourself can take much longer and you may get lost along the way.

7 Whatever the cause, make sure that you work through it until you are able to release it and it is no longer an issue. Remember that there is a huge difference between releasing anger and suppressing it. It's the difference between being healed and keeping a festering wound unseen to.

I want to share with you one last thought. No matter what happens to you, you always have a choice of how you will think about something and how you will react to it. It's up to you whether you cling to your angry feelings or whether you decide to release them. Clinging

> 'Suppressed anger and emotion is like a volcano which builds up'

to them will only result in hurting you further and it gives your power away to the person or event that made you angry. If you want to be truly free and at peace you need to feel the anger and then let it go.

 48 Coping with change

'Last week I found out that Dad has been offered a job overseas and I'm terrified of all the changes this will bring: a new country, city and school. It also means that I'll be leaving all my friends, my pets and my house. How will I cope? What if I don't make any new friends? Should I try to change his mind? I lie awake at night worrying about all the changes that frighten me...'

As Confucius said: 'Only one thing is certain in life and that is that things will change.' How would you define your approach to change? Do you welcome every opportunity for changing or do you resist, hoping that your world will remain the same?

Now, far more than ever before, change is a part of our lives. Some of us are great at handling change and others resist it with all their might. Change faces us from our earliest years. In our teens we could be changing schools, starting college or work, moving to a new city or country, losing a friend who wants to spend all her time with her boyfriend, or we might even find ourselves changing as people. As we get older the type of change we encounter may be different, but there will inevitably be similar aspects which are age-independent.

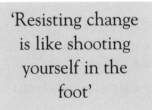

'Resisting change is like shooting yourself in the foot'

Why we fear change

Many of us might, at some stage, find ourselves afraid of the change we're facing and it's at times like these that understanding what's happening can be really helpful. The more you understand what change is about, the better you'll be able to cope with it and the easier life will be for you. Here are some of the truths about change:

✳ Change is often essential, even if it's painful. (If caterpillars resisted change there'd be no butterflies.)

✳ We're frightened by change because we're comfortable with what we know and we're afraid of the unknown.

✳ Being comfortable means feeling safe. Confronting something new throws us out of our comfort zone.

✳ Sometimes, if we've had a lot of change as children, especially if it was negative change, as we get older we resist further change. It's our way of protecting ourselves from what we think threatens us.

✳ Resisting change is a bit like shooting yourself in the foot. It can backfire on you.

✳ Some change isn't positive. If you're able to avoid it then do so. If you can't, then look for the best option.

✳ Sometimes it's good to initiate change. It gives your life fresh spin.

✳ The opposite of change can be stagnation.

✳ Don't just change for change's sake, always know why you're trying to do something.

✳ When faced with change, take steps towards it. This gives you power and control over it and stops you feeling helpless.

✳ If change is scary, feel the fear and then face it. The taller we stand the smaller it seems.

✳ Change usually brings opportunity.

If you're worried about the change coming your way, there are a number of steps you can take to help you through whatever it is that you are facing:

1 Identify what the change is (a new school, moving house, a loss, an opportunity, your parents' divorce, a job).

2 Understand why it's happening.

3 See if you can influence what's happening or whether it is being forced onto you.

If you can influence what's happening:

✳ See what options you have.

✳ List the pros and cons for each option.

☀ Pick the best option.

☀ Adopt a mindset that's positive and enthusiastic, and try to look forward to the change.

☀ Be involved in implementing the option you've settled on.

☀ If you encounter hiccups, look for the best solution and move forward.

☀ Make the best of your new situation. If you're not happy with the outcome, see what you or anyone else could do to improve the circumstances you're in.

If you're unable to influence the change:

☀ See if there is any other approach that could be taken which would be less worrying for you.

☀ If there's no other way out, adopt a positive mindset and approach the situation constructively. Look at everything from two sides, namely, what will the outcome be if you:

  – resist the change and sink into negative thoughts?

  – approach things positively and work towards the best outcome?

☀ Try to apply the second approach. The first one is a sure way to unhappiness. This doesn't mean that the second one is guaranteed to make you happy, but it's the only way towards achieving the best outcome possible.

4 Don't look at change as your enemy. Treat it like a friend and try to look forward to what it will bring.

An excellent description about how to approach change can be found in the book *Who Moved My Cheese?* by Dr Spencer Johnson. It's well worth reading as it is short, simple, puts it all so well and probably applies to nearly every one of us. Change, in today's world, is one of the factors that contributes greatly to the stress levels we experience, so anything that helps us cope better with it is worth a look.

'If change is scary, feel the fear and then face it'

49 Making a difficult choice

'My best friend's boyfriend has started taking drugs and now he's drawing her into his circle of drug-taking friends. I've told her about my concerns, but she scoffs at them and makes fun of me for not wanting to join in. Yesterday she told me that if I don't change my attitude we should stop being friends. What should I do? I don't want to lose my best friend, but I also don't want anything to do with the drug scene...'

Difficult choices are those where you stand to lose something if you make the wrong choice. Sometimes you might stand to lose something whichever way you choose. Those are the hardest choices.

10 steps to making a hard decision

When you're faced with a difficult decision, think about the following:

1 Why do you feel you have to make a decision?
2 What are your options?
3 List the pros and cons of each option.
4 Are you making a decision because someone else wants you to do so, if so, why?
5 What will happen if you don't make a decision?
6 What does your gut-feeling tell you?
7 Does one of the options involve doing something wrong, dishonest or immoral? (Sticking to your values makes decision-making much easier.)
8 Do you want to make a decision based on emotion or on logic?
9 Which option will have the most positive impact on your life in say, ten years' time?
10 Which option is best for you? (Not for anyone else. For you.)

Write down the answers and study them. See if you can now make a decision. If you are able to make a decision at this point, then go about your normal activities and every now and again check with yourself that you're happy with the decision.

If you find you are still unable to make the decision, then it's good to ask someone else. Selecting whom you ask is important. Do you just want someone who will listen to your problem, enabling you to then make a decision? Or do you want someone who can give you advice and help you with the decision-making? It's good to approach someone who is in a position to help, or who knows a process which will help you. Make sure you know whether this person has something at stake in your decision-making so that you know if he or she is being completely objective in the advice.

> 'The hardest choices are those where you stand to lose something whichever way you choose'

It's important to listen to others' opinions and then to make the decision that feels good for you. Always remember that it's your life and you have to live with and be comfortable with your choice.

50 When you've made a mistake

'The other day, while I was at my aunt's house, I knocked over her favourite porcelain horse and it broke into little pieces. I was terrified of what her reaction might be. I panicked, and I swept up the pieces and threw them in the bin, hoping that it would be some time before she noticed the horse was missing. Unfortunately she did notice and she's convinced that the plumber must have stolen it while he was fixing a tap. Now my aunt, who has a reputation for being fierce, is meeting the owner of the plumbing company and will demand retribution. I know that what I did was wrong, and that it could cost someone's job, but I'm petrified of what my aunt might do if I own up...'

There are times when we all do something we regret. Doing or saying something dishonest is one of those, but there are many others. When you feel you've made a mistake, you have three primary choices:

☀ You can realise what you've done, shrug it off as not serious and just carry on.
☀ You can let the severity of what you've done overwhelm you with a sense of guilt and fear, eventually affecting your whole life and making you dislike yourself.
☀ You can admit to yourself what it is that you did wrong and then work on a plan for what to do next and how to fix it.

It may seem obvious that the third option is the best one, but surprisingly it often isn't as easy as that. It depends on what it is you did, how serious the implications are, whether it involved other people, whether anyone got hurt by what you did and also your reason for doing it.

Work out why you did it

It's important to understand why you did what you did. If you don't take the time to do this you'll probably find yourself doing the same type of thing again. To learn from your mistakes, it's important to understand what made you do it and why. Sometimes the answer is simple. You made a small mistake, became afraid of the implications and proceeded to make ever bigger mistakes in your endeavours to cover it up. Perhaps you didn't know how to undo your initial mistake and you just blundered on. Perhaps you did one major thing wrong and became paralysed by fear.

It is actually essential to stop in your tracks as soon as you've made the first mistake. Stop, ask yourself why you did what you did and then see what you can do to correct it. Sometimes there is nothing you can do about what is now in the past, but you can always make sure that your next step is the best possible one. If you don't do this you can inadvertently embark on a path where you are silencing your conscience and explaining away to yourself why it is OK to do what you are doing. If it's wrong or dishonest, it's never OK.

'The effort involved in doing things right is ultimately always less than if you continue doing more things wrong'

The analogy of walking along a slippery, icy river bank always appeals to me. Your first dishonesty is like a small slip down the bank. A small slip is still easy to recover from. You realise what happened, grab onto something and pull yourself up. If, as you try to get up, you slip again, you slide further down. Sometimes it may even seem easier to just let go and slide all the way down. The further you slide the harder it is to clamber back up to the top. It may even seem impossible.

Life is like that walk along the river bank. You can't expect never to slip, but it's what you do next that is so important. Sometimes the actions you need to take to put yourself back on the right track may seem harder than taking the easy way out. You may need great courage and strength to do the right thing. One thing that is for sure, no matter where you are and how much effort it will take to start doing things right, that effort is always less than what you'll need if you let yourself continue doing more things wrong.

It's never too late to stop in your tracks. You may need help in understanding why and how you went wrong and in what to do to put things right. Ask for that help. Don't stop asking until you know what it is you have to do and then go and do it. Don't ever give up and accept that you're destined to fail. You may not be able to turn the clock back or to undo what has happened, but you can always choose what you will do next.

You are the only person truly responsible for your life and you can always choose your direction. Do what is right for you, not just what is easiest.

51 Temptation

'Exams start next week and, in spite of having worked fairly steadily, I still feel unsure of my work. Yesterday I walked into the secretary's office just as she was putting the exam papers away into a file in her cabinet. I've been given the job of photocopying and I know that I'll be working alone in her office over the next two days. I now can't get that file out of my mind. Do I wait until I know that she will be out of her office, and then quickly make a copy of the relevant papers? Or do I remain steadfast and resist the urge? Knowing the questions would make my revision so much easier...'

What is temptation? It's when someone (or something) entices you to do something you know is wrong. What should you do when it happens? No doubt you know the answer and no doubt you say 'Resist'. If we know what we should do, why then do we so often give in to the temptation?

We give in because we're not as strong as we'd like to be. The weaker we are the easier it is to succumb. We're also very clever at convincing ourselves that what we're doing is actually OK. The more we want it, the more creative our justifications. Does this sound at all familiar? We'll even lie outright to ourselves (and to others). Furthermore, we can convince ourselves so thoroughly that we end up believing ourselves. Then we're not lying anymore, are we? We're just doing what we feel is right. Wrong! Putting a blindfold on your eyes doesn't mean you're blind.

What, then, is the answer? It's a tough one. The only option is to remind yourself about the right thing to do – and then to do it. You need to dredge up every ounce of strength you didn't even know you had and you need to stand firm.

What helps, as you realise you're being tempted, is to stop yourself in your tracks and ask yourself a few questions:

☀ Why is whatever's tempting you so attractive?
☀ What benefits will it bring you?
☀ Why shouldn't you do it?

☀ What does your gut-feeling tell you?

☀ Do you really think the price you'll pay will be worth it, even in the long run?

☀ How easy will it be to undo what you're about to do?

☀ Even if no-one else knows what you've done, what will it do to your self-respect?

☀ If you don't do this, will you really be much worse off?

☀ Is there anything else you can do which will satisfy your need and won't be wrong?

> 'Putting a blindfold on doesn't mean you're blind'

Then contemplate your answers.

Working up the strength to resist

Temptations obviously come in varying degrees of seriousness. The more serious the 'wrong' you're tempted by, the more you should think it over. To give yourself strength, there are some tactics you can employ:

☀ Share your dilemma with someone who has sound values and hear her or his advice.

☀ Remind yourself that deep down you are a quality individual, no matter what you or others may think. As that quality individual, the road you want to take should go up and not down.

☀ Know that by the very fact that you're aware of your temptation, you're already gaining strength. Build on that strength.

☀ Visualise yourself turning away from the temptation. Feel the strength flood your body and mind. Feel the satisfaction in your heart and the sense of achievement.

☀ Congratulate yourself and walk away feeling proud of the way you handled it. The easiest way is to turn away as soon as you realize you're being tempted by something that isn't right. The further you go, the harder it is to turn back.

May your life be free of difficult temptations – and if you can't be free from them, may you be filled with much courage and strength to do the right thing.

52 Smoking, drinking and drugs

'My Mum doesn't like the fact that many of the friends I hang out with smoke – and many of them drink too. I don't smoke or drink, and I don't want to start. When I leave school I'll have the odd social drink, but I've seen how people behave when they're drunk and I never want to be out of control like that. Why do my friends do it? What could get them to change?'

Smoking. Drinking. Drugs. These are real-life issues that are bound to confront you at some time – and the more you've thought about them beforehand the better prepared you'll be. What are your current thoughts and standpoints concerning these matters? Here is my perspective on them:

Smoking

If you look at it objectively, the attraction for cigarettes is very hard to understand. Those of us who grew up with parents who smoke will know all about living in a haze of smoke and will no doubt have witnessed the numerous, usually futile, attempts at giving up. Friends who smoke usually say they started their habit because they wanted to look cool. What they don't realise is that they don't actually look cool – and what's even worse is that they smell definitely uncool.

If you ever try smoking you'll never again really know what you smell like. It's odd, but it quickly seems to affect your own sense of smell and taste and masks the effects. Someone who smokes is blissfully unaware that they, their hair and their clothes have this stale, smoky stench. Their breath is also enough to make others recoil, but you politely keep an unflinching look on your face so as not to offend them. Some of their teeth sometimes go yellow and, as for kissing a smoker, it is quite justifiably compared to licking the proverbial ashtray.

Does all this sound cool to you? Aside from the fact that smoking is ultimately good for boosting sales of deodorant, perfumes, gum and toothpaste (necessary for covering up and trying to undo unpleasant side effects), all other spin-offs are negative. Some of the short-term effects of smoking are that it:

※ makes your hair and clothes smell
※ stains your teeth
※ gives you bad breath
※ makes your skin dry
※ causes wrinkles earlier in life
※ can affect your sports performance – you won't be able to run as fast or as far.

It also causes a lot of serious and often fatal diseases, such as:

※ coronary heart disease
※ emphysema
※ mouth cancer
※ throat cancer
※ lung cancer
※ bladder cancer.

When you're young, health risks seem so intangible, but you quickly hit reality if you witness someone dying from smoking-related heart disease, cancer or emphysema. You hit reality even harder if it's you who's dying.

Smoking, being addictive, is also very hard to stop once you've started. The amount of effort, and expense, that many people undertake in order to give up what they realise is a destructive habit is worth taking note of. More often than not they fail anyway. Some girls take up smoking in the mistaken belief that it will keep their weight down and they don't realise the risks they're taking on, and the damage they're doing to themselves.

Another aspect which is usually ignored by those who smoke is the effect their smoke has on the non-smokers around them. Not only is the secondary smoke the others inhale bad for them, but it's altogether a very unpleasant experience for them. So often, to be polite or to avoid confrontation, they put up with discomfort in silence.

If you're still intent on smoking, ask yourself what benefits it will bring you. Then ask yourself whether it may not be better to be really cool, look good, smell attractive, have extra money, be healthy and be great to kiss? Leave the smelly stuff for those who don't care about such things.

Drinking

Under the right circumstances and in limited quantities, an alcoholic beverage (drunk by adults) can be a pleasant refreshment or an enjoyable accompaniment to a good meal. The word 'can' is key here. Not everyone experiences pleasant effects, not everyone limits it to one glass and not everyone waits until she or he is an adult.

Many teenagers try alcohol, and when they do they are courting serious danger, danger they probably don't even see. It usually starts with trying to impress friends or as an attempt to dull some inner painful feeling. It may initially sound like a good idea, but it backfires fast.

Nowadays, with greater awareness of the harmful effects of drug use, drinking seems an increasingly 'cool' thing to do. There will be times when you may even find yourself mocked, scorned or ridiculed if you refuse an alcoholic drink. Be strong and resist it, it's your best and only truly viable option. Those who try to entice you to drink remind me of the old story of the frog in the well:

> There once was a frog who fell into a deep well. He was cold, stiff and
> scared. When his friends gathered around the rim to see what had happened,
> he called to them to join him. He enticed them with descriptions of amazing
> warmth and happiness. Eventually they believed him and jumped in. Only
> then did they realise what an awful, lonely and scary place the well was.
> They understood then that there was no way out and that their only source
> of comfort was to entice other frogs into the well for company. They all
> gathered together and called out to any frog who came close to the well.

Teenagers who drink, as well as those people who abuse alcohol, are somewhat like those frogs in the well. They take pleasure in luring others into adopting their destructive behaviour.

Other than when it's appropriately used – on occasion, by adults, socially, in controlled quantities – alcohol brings a range of problematic effects:

* **It can temporarily fool you into thinking that all your troubles have gone**. While you are in this 'happy' state, those who haven't drunk anything see you quite differently. They see someone who undergoes a personality change, becomes unavailable, cannot grasp what is being said, acts silly or aggressively, thinks she is being funny, loses control of her actions and sometimes goes so far as to vomit and pass out.

* **By losing control over yourself you make yourself vulnerable** to doing things you would normally never do. You might try things which suddenly seem exciting, such as drugs or sex. You might even feel capable of driving and you're likely to insist on it even if others try to dissuade you.

* **Driving seems to be one skill that a drunk person thinks she or he will always have**. People who have drunk too much will insist they're alright, they'll even take passengers and they'll risk their own and others' lives. For what? Can anything be worth it if the risk is that you might kill or maim someone? This unfortunately is a reality that happens every day.

* **You expose yourself to the risk of being taken advantage of**. Many incidents of date rape, abuse or theft occur when the victim is in an inebriated state.

* **Abused regularly, alcohol kills off brain cells**, leaving you with a reduced ability to learn and work.

* **On average, the female body doesn't cope** with the volumes of alcohol a male body can. We get drunk because our livers can't metabolise alcohol as quickly. Many teen girls try to keep up with their male friends and quickly become so drunk that they no longer know how awful they look and how badly they're behaving. Scenes of girls throwing up and passing out are not uncommon in today's clubs.

* **When you sober up after being drunk, you feel awful**. You'll probably have a bad headache, you'll be nauseous and generally feel unwell. You may struggle to remember what you did while you were drunk and you'll

feel awkward about facing those who were with you.

☀ **Alcohol can easily drag you into a vicious circle** of feeling that you need more to feel better. Your body may start to crave some of the ingredients, you stop thinking clearly and you fool yourself into believing that if you have some more it'll fix your problems. Once you get caught in this scary cycle it's very hard to get out. You are an alcoholic. You feel that you're only OK if you've had a drink, your self-esteem melts away, you may realise that you have a problem, but you feel totally helpless. Your only hope of clawing yourself back to a healthy and normal life is to get urgent assistance. If you don't, you're in serious danger of jeopardising your entire life.

☀ **Those people who become reliant on alcohol don't only harm themselves**, they harm all the relationships around them. Whether they become abusive, morose or simply unavailable, they cannot avoid affecting and causing great pain to those who are close to them. They end up destroying the most important aspects of their lives.

Could anything be worth exposing yourself to these 'effects'? It doesn't mean that no-one should ever drink. There's a time and a place when, as an adult, having a social drink may be a very pleasant experience. (The emphasis here is on the word 'social' as it is never a good idea to drink alone.) Some scientists even say that a glass of wine a day can help to keep people healthier. The important message is that it's not worth risking any of the effects described earlier by starting too young or drinking too much. Why risk your whole future, your happiness and your relationships? Be strong – you'll thank yourself one day.

Drugs

When you try drugs you're gambling with your life. You can take all of the effects listed about alcohol, multiply them a hundredfold and add to them the guarantee that you will significantly damage your life. You may think that you might try drugs just once, but you can never know what will happen to you. There are a few people who have managed to try a drug once and never again. They are in a tiny minority. The rest get caught up in a nightmare that lasts for the rest of their lives.

You've got your whole future ahead of you. You can maximise on the talents you've been given and, if you want to, you can achieve so much. Don't throw it all away for a brief and misguided sensation that will destroy your mind and your body. Anyone who tells you that drugs won't have serious and permanent side effects is lying to you. All the scientific evidence proves that there is brain damage of some sort – from lasting paranoia to memory loss. And that's at the mild end of the scale. The social costs are huge, from your family disowning you, to friends refusing to have anything to do with you, to not being able to hold down a job and

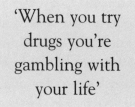

'When you try drugs you're gambling with your life'

therefore facing a life, probably a short one, of destitution. And your addiction makes you vulnerable to prostitution.

If you find that you're being lured into trying a drug, stop dead in your tracks and don't move until you are certain that you can defy the temptation. Read Chapter 51 on Temptation, seek help and support from someone who is strong enough and who is qualified to help you, and do *everything* to resist.

When it comes to deciding about drugs, the only time you can think clearly is when you haven't tried one. After that, you'll never again be free to make an objective decision. While you have that total freedom, make the choice that will allow you to keep that freedom forever. Say 'No!'

53 When you need help

'My parents got divorced last year. After the initial shock and break-up of our family unit things slowly settled down and it seemed that life would be OK after all. Then Dad got involved with a woman who doesn't like me and now I hardly see him. Mum's very busy at work and relies on me to look after the house and my younger brothers. I'm at lectures all day, then I shop for what we need, make dinner, put the boys to bed and only then I settle down to study. I never have time for my friends, I'm tired all the time and I don't know what to do…'

There will inevitably be times when you may feel you are stuck, when you don't have the answers, when you don't know what to do, when you're lost, lonely or sad. When you know that you, on your own, are not enough. That is the time to seek help.

Think through your situation so that you understand clearly the need or the problem. Then think of someone who has the ability to provide you with a solution, an answer, some support, or even just sympathy, understanding or love.

Turning to the right person is so important, someone who has your needs genuinely at heart, someone who truly cares about the outcome of your situation, someone who honestly wants to see you happy. That someone may be your mother, a good friend, your life's companion, a relation, or someone whose chosen profession is to help others (a priest, a doctor or a counsellor).

'To ask for help is to acknowledge that involvement from another person will bring improvement'

It is important to accept that you cannot do everything on your own, and then to reach out for help. To ask for help is not an admission of failure. It is an acknowledgement that involvement from another person will bring an improvement. It is a sign that you are strong enough to realise the difficulty you have and that you have the strength to do something about it. Sometimes it will be easy to know whom to reach out to, and at other times it may be hard.

I hope that someone close will always be around for you, to talk to, to share your problems, worries or joys with, to listen when you have something to say, to advise wisely when you seek guidance. May there always be a pillar of support for you, a source of strength for you to draw from, a haven of peace from life's turbulent storms.

May you always find the help you need, through talking, through doing, through reading and by finding what is right for you.

54 Feeling lonely or alone

'My family recently left the town where I'd grown up and now we've come to a city I've never even been to before. I've left all my friends back home and I don't know anyone at this huge new school I'm at. The kids here are quite aloof and they all have their own friends. My brother is away at college, Mum and Dad both work long hours, and I spend a lot of time alone. I eat breakfast alone, sit in silence on the bus, eat my lunch alone and come home to an empty house. I've tried chatting to the other kids, but after a few words they turn to talk to someone else. I'm feeling very down and seem to have no energy left, so all my time at home is spent sleeping or watching TV. I so wish we could go back to our old home…'

There are times in your life when you will suddenly feel lonely or very alone. We all have them. As a child, as a teenager and even as an adult, we sometimes feel alone. There is a difference between being lonely and alone, but I'll deal with them together. The good news is that this feeling does pass, sometimes sooner, sometimes later – but while you're in it life can feel somewhat hard.

Finding the reason

You can find yourself feeling alone for a variety of different reasons. Before you can do something about it, it's important that you identify why you feel the way you do.

Has something happened? Have you had a fight with a friend? Did you get into trouble over something? Are you afraid of something you still have to face? Have you lost someone close? Do you just feel different to the others around you, as if you don't fit in? Are you carrying a secret burden or fear or guilt that you can't share with anyone? Are you lacking in confidence or coping ability? Are you new to the area?

Whatever the reason, when you feel alone it can be quite a scary feeling. You probably don't know how to get out of it or how long it'll take. What makes it worse is if no-one else seems to understand what you're feeling. If they tease you or abandon you it makes things even harder.

Thinking things through

The best thing to do when you are in this lonely state is to take some time to think everything through. Understand the reason for feeling the way you do – and the stuff behind the reason. For example, you may be feeling alone because you somehow don't fit into your group of friends. Try to understand why it is that you don't fit in. Is it because they're smarter than you, cooler than you, doing things you don't agree with?

What can you do to change things?

Once you know the reasons, see what you can do to change things. Some reasons will be easy to overcome and others may be more complicated.

※ List all the ideas that come to you and at this stage don't reject any.
※ Have a brain-storming session with yourself, talking to yourself as if helping a friend.
※ If there's someone you can trust, someone you can turn to, then include him or her in this exercise.
※ Let all your creative juices flow and don't be afraid to come up with crazy-sounding ideas.
※ Now examine each idea and have some fun seeing if it could work. See if it's possible. Does it ring true in terms of your values? Don't consider things if they feel wrong in your value system. In your imagination, follow the idea through to a happy and positive outcome. Does it feel good? If so, put it down on the 'to do' list. Is there someone you would like to involve in the idea? Is there something you need to get, learn or do in order for the idea to work?

Taking action

Sometimes the answer will simply lie in being patient and waiting for some event you already know of to happen. Even then there may well be something you can do in the meantime to lighten your spirit. At other times you may need to work hard at the items you've put down on your 'to do' list. Just deciding on a goal and putting an action plan in place is often enough to make you feel less lonely and more positive about life.

Some of your solutions may take time. If you want to make new friends or address an unhappy family situation, you need ideas and a plan of how to get to where you want to be. Such issues can be hard to tackle on your own, so the first step is to see who could help you.

Having a good friend that you can trust and have fun with is one of the best ways of easing loneliness. Becoming involved in activities is a good way to make friends and it gives you something to work towards. Whether it's an activity like a sport, art, music, photography or drama, it gives you something to do and an opportunity to meet others your age. Choose activities that attract people you can relate to and who have similar values to yours.

> 'Being comfortable with just ourselves for company can be good for us'

Once you're taking part in the activity, try really hard to be as positive and enthusiastic as possible. Even if you don't feel positive, by forcing yourself to be outgoing and friendly you'll be making it easier for others to be drawn to you. You'll also eventually absorb the positive approach and it will begin to come naturally. If you still find it hard to make friends with the others in your group, then focus on enjoying the activity and get satisfaction from what you're doing. Friendship is bound to develop eventually, somehow, somewhere.

A different approach

Another approach is to see your state of aloneness in a different light. More so now than before, life can be constantly abuzz with activity, noise and social interaction. This situation quite often leads to girls becoming heavily dependant on their friends and on the constant presence of others around them, so much so that they find it very hard to spend time alone. Next time you find yourself alone, try to treasure the time you have to yourself.

Write in your journal, read a book, do some sketching, try a new recipe, perhaps phone an elderly person you haven't spoken to for a while – and enjoy your own company. One of life's key skills, and one which helps to set us up for coping with life's challenges, is the ability to be alone. Becoming too reliant on always being surrounded by others takes away some of your confidence and sense of self. It also robs you of those quiet, introspective times, times which allow you to know and understand yourself, your values and your dreams. This doesn't mean that you now become a loner or hermit, but it does mean that being comfortable with just yourself for company can be good for you.

Your options

When you feel alone you have two options available to you. You can choose to let yourself sink into an increasingly glum state, or you can decide to focus on all the positives in your life and pull yourself up by your boot-straps. This can be easier said than done, but there's something you should always try to remember: you may not be able to help being in your situation, but you can always choose what you're going to do about it. Focusing on the positives is always very powerful.

May your life be filled with love, companionship, support and peace in your heart – and may you embrace the moments of solitude you encounter as you walk along life's path.

55 Breaking up

'Simon and I have been dating for nearly two years and all along I've suspected that my feelings for him were stronger than his for me. He would often say cruel things to me when he was angry, but then he'd apologize and assure me that I was the girl he wanted to be with. A couple of weeks ago everything changed. He started criticising me all the time and became sullen and withdrawn. Then, a week ago, he said he was in love with another girl, and he was breaking up with me. How could he do this to me? Why now, just after we'd become more physically intimate? I can't bear the thought of running into him at lectures – in fact I can't bear the thought of seeing anyone right now...'

As the song says, 'Breaking up is hard to do'. No kidding! Breaking up a relationship with someone is one of those tough moments in life. If someone is breaking up with you it can feel as if your whole world is collapsing. When you break up with someone, depending on how much you care for that person, it can be almost as painful.

Breaking up can mean floods of tears for days on end, tears and grief for the loss of the friendship, for the fact that you probably won't be seeing your friend again and out of fear of the loneliness you will have to face. There might even be times when you cry so hard that those around you won't know what to do with you. Then, slowly, you get over it. That old cliché, 'time is the best healer', is actually very true, even though it can be hard to understand when you're in the middle of heartbreak.

Why break up?

Sometimes it feels as if it would be much easier to just continue with the relationship, but what may seem easier doesn't actually work out for the best. Read Chapter 24, When You Don't Love Him, for some more detailed thoughts about why you might break up a relationship. If a relationship isn't working, tough as it may be, it's better to end it. At times, the fear of hurting your boyfriend's feelings can cloud your judgement, but staying with him for the wrong reasons can ultimately be more cruel than being honest upfront. Depending on how you do it, you might even end up staying friends. Friendship may be hard at first as the wounds are still quite raw, but with time you may find that the aspects you liked in each other are still there and being friends is the best option.

When is it the right thing to do?

How do you know if you should break things off? Some situations will be very clear. Something may have happened, he may have found someone else or you just don't like him anymore. Your heart tells you what you need to do and, armed with some courage and the right words, you break up. He may take it badly and you may be very upset, but deep down you know you're doing the right thing.

What if you're unsure about what to do? Asking yourself some important questions can be very helpful:

✳ What has led you to thinking of breaking up?
✳ What will happen if you just continue with the relationship?
✳ Are you in love with him?
✳ Is he a good person? Does he treat you with respect? Is he honest, kind, trustworthy?
✳ What attracted you to him in the first place? Is that aspect still there?

If you're really honest with yourself, your heart will tell you what's the right thing to do. Try always to listen to your heart and your gut-feeling because they are seldom wrong. Sometimes your head tries to contradict your heart. You do need to listen to your head too, but most importantly you need to make the decision that is best for you.

When you ought to break up with him

If you're involved with someone who breaks the law or your moral code, you need to get out while you can. If he drinks, is abusive or takes drugs, you stand an almost zero chance of changing him. You can ask him to stop and if he wants to he will. If he doesn't, all you can do is ask him to seek professional help. Even if he stops there's a good chance he might start up again. Being with someone like that can be extremely destructive for you. You can easily get caught up in his problems and eventually develop ones of your own. If he's abusive towards you, don't waste any more time and get out now! You should never tolerate being with someone who doesn't respect you as it will eventually undermine your overall self-esteem and happiness.

It is essential that you do not lose sight of the special person that you are. You are unique, you have talents and strengths and you must respect yourself to ensure that others will respect you too. You were born with a beautiful heart and one of your top priorities is to ensure that it stays beautiful. You deserve to be treated as the special person you are and you must never allow yourself to be abused by anyone, either physically or emotionally.

Other factors

Not all relationships involve issues as serious as those I've mentioned. Some just don't work. It may be that you're just incompatible, you fight incessantly or there's simply no chemistry between you. If it's not working it's best to admit the truth and to move on. Let love and common sense be your guide and don't let fear hold you back.

Sometimes, even though you know that breaking up is what you should do, it's very hard to actually do it. Throwing yourself into something new can be a way of providing you with the extra strength you need to break up. By taking up something new and making new friends, even going on a new date, you reduce your need to rely on a relationship that isn't working.

This does not mean for one minute that you turn into a cold, hard person who uses others for her own interests. The assumption is that you're always acting from a sense of integrity and that your genuine intention is to do the best in terms of yourself while considering the other person's feelings. If you have love in your heart, for yourself, for others, for life – then your actions will be driven by a sense of fairness and concern for all involved. All the advice here is given keeping your interests at heart and is meant to help you through what can be a very hard experience.

When he breaks up with you

The other side of breaking up is when someone breaks up with you and it's not what you want. I have said quite a bit about this in Chapter 25, When He Doesn't Love You. It's very painful knowing that someone doesn't want you or like you the way you want him. Depending on your relationship, breaking up can be painful for different reasons. If you're in love with him, the pain is about loss, about rejection, about grief and about not knowing if you'll ever find someone like that again.

If you don't love him, the pain can be more about your damaged ego and pride. It hurts to know that someone doesn't want to be with you and it can really shake you up. This is a bit easier to recover from and it needs a good dose of telling yourself that it wouldn't have worked out anyway and this is

'If a relationship isn't working it's better to end it'

for the best. Try to let go of your anger so it doesn't fester inside you, causing continual damage. If you do feel angry, read Chapter 47 on Anger as it's important to work through it and release the anger you feel.

Coping with the loss

If the break-up has been really devastating for you, try not to go through it all on your own. See who you could turn to for support and loving empathy. Coping with loss is much harder to do if you're alone and often it's just the presence of an interested and compassionate listener that can make a big difference. You need to be able to share your pain and it certainly isn't a sign of weakness if you need someone to help you through it all. When you're really struggling, asking for help is the best choice you can make. Read When You Need Help, Chapter 53, for more thoughts about this.

After a painful break-up, the one thought that's usually very helpful is: 'This obviously wasn't meant to be, perhaps for reasons that are unclear to me now – and I must now concentrate on doing everything possible to cope and to look forward to a better, happier relationship one day in the future.'

May some of these words help your heart through the challenges life may throw you on your journey.

56 Divorce

'My friend Sheryl's parents have just announced that they're getting a divorce. Sheryl knew that they fought a lot, but she never expected them to divorce and now she is completely heartbroken. She also feels she is partly to blame because many of the fights were about money and the cost of her sporting activities. Sheryl is a great sportswoman and excels in ballet, gymnastics and show-jumping. She suggested to her parents that she give up her riding and ballet, but they say their divorce has nothing to do with the cost of Sheryl's sport. Sheryl is so desperately sad and I wish I could do something to help...'

This dreaded word is unfortunately becoming heard more and more frequently. It used to affect someone we'd heard of, then someone we knew and now it sometimes touches our own lives.

It is not your fault

What is so important for you to remember is that no matter what happens, it is *never* the child's fault. As a child it may seem as if there is something you could have done to prevent the divorce from happening. There wasn't, isn't and won't ever be anything a child can do. It's an adult thing. It's about the parents and the relationship they share.

Divorce happens because those two adults who once loved each other and dreamed of being together forever now no longer want to be together. Relationships are complicated and they need a lot of wisdom and hard work to survive the inevitable ups and downs. Sometimes, despite best intentions, things go wrong.

Something a child may never know is how terribly hard divorce is for most parents who go through it. It is devastating for the child, but it can be surprisingly hard for the parents. Depending on the circumstances, the pain can sometimes border on the unbearable. Maybe one parent feels the pain more, but no-one goes unscathed.

First there is the pain of realising that the marriage is in trouble. The shattering of the dream and the disbelief that this could be happening brings on a state of shock and grief. Then there may be attempts to fix things, followed by the realisation that they cannot be repaired. Some marriages do succeed here, they manage to overcome their difficulties and they stay together for the rest of their days. I'm talking about those unfortunate ones that fail.

The pain that leads up to actually making that decision is hard to describe. It involves so many different aspects. The biggest pain comes from knowing the hurt that is inevitable for the children. Ask any mother and, with a few extraordinary exceptions, she'll tell you that her child is the centre of her world. The love a mother has for the child she carried inside her for so long is hard to understand without being a mother oneself. I'm not minimising the love a father has, I'm just speaking here from a mother's perspective.

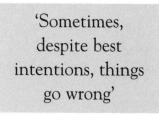

'Sometimes, despite best intentions, things go wrong'

The child the mother brings into the world is so precious to her she would give up her life for it should the need arise. She cares for her child, always doing what she believes to be best for this child she so loves and now she is about to do something which will bring her child untold pain.

The knowledge that she will cause this hurt to the person she loves so much puts her through turmoil, guilt, pain, desperation and grief. These feelings may not always occur as severely for everyone, but they're true in many cases. Divorce can sometimes feel worse than losing a loved one through death. What makes it so bad for the parents is the knowledge that they are totally responsible for what is happening. It is knowing that their own decisions, mistakes and circumstances have led to this. The child is the innocent victim of adult mistakes.

A very human mistake

Some parents, during this time of pain and turmoil, may not seem as if they love their children the way they're supposed to. This is only because they themselves are caught up in such grief, blame and anger that they don't act completely 'normally'. They may be angry with their spouse, with themselves and with their circumstances. They may feel as if they're falling apart inside, that they won't cope with what they're going through and yet, as parents, they're supposed to be strong and do all the right things.

An important fact to be aware of is that, as parents, we are still human. We are far from perfect. We make mistakes. We also have times when we may feel vulnerable, inadequate and frightened. We're often expected to act like Superman, but the problem is that we're just normal humans.

In some cases, divorce may even be the best solution. If the love has gone and a relationship becomes destructive, or if there's abuse involved, then there's not much else to be done. Sometimes the parents know that if they stay together it may be worse for the children in the long-run. These are the hard decisions and no-one really has all the answers. Everyone involved stumbles around, hoping that what they're doing is the best thing.

I hope you never have to experience any of this as it definitely is one of the hardest things to go through. If anyone you know gets caught up in a divorce, be there for him or her and stress that it is never his or her fault. It's an adult issue and the adults must sort it out between themselves. I would also suggest that your friend sees a therapist because this is one experience that is very hard to go through without help.

May the light shine bright inside you, may it give you strength to face all of life's challenges and may you have the good fortune to be surrounded by love all the days of your life.

57 when someone close dies

'Four days ago my best friend Julie drowned. She and some friends were swimming in the sea and no-one quite knows what happened, but she disappeared under a large wave and by the time someone realised there was a problem, it was too late. My whole world feels as if it has collapsed around me. We were so close and now she's gone forever. I can't believe that this has happened, that we'll never laugh, or hug, or share secrets with each other again. I don't know how to cope with this – I don't think I'll ever be the same again…'

Death is so final. For those left behind it is an end, the closing of a chapter. This is something many of us struggle with and there are no easy answers, but there are certain feelings you inevitably go through, and others that give comfort – so let's look at them and perhaps they'll bring you comfort too.

The emotions that follow loss

First comes the shock, the horror of what has happened. Then the refusal to accept that this can be so. Then comes an awful sense of aloneness. This person that you knew is gone. There is no-one else who knew you in that way, no-one who shared with you those experiences and discussions. This is usually the time when you cry for yourself and for what you have lost.

Then you may experience a sense of guilt. This seems to be a common feeling, but it's very hard none the less. You feel guilt that if only you had done something differently, spent more time with the person, been kinder, hadn't said some of those things. Some people even feel guilt at their own reaction to the death.

You may also feel angry, for various reasons that sound crazy, and yet it is a feeling that can arrive out of the blue. You may be angry with the person for leaving you, for letting you down, for the pain you're going through. This feeling doesn't always occur, but if it does it's important to understand it for what it is, to feel it and then let it go.

It is important to let yourself feel all those feelings that come like waves from the ocean. Don't suppress them and pretend they're not there. That's a sure way of pushing them down for some time, but they're also sure to come back in some other, even harder way.

When you let yourself feel the feelings and then think about them, you can get to understand them and why they're there. Sometimes if they're very difficult it's good to talk them through with someone who understands, perhaps a close friend or even a counsellor. Talking about them helps to release them and allows you to accept that it's OK to feel pain. It can also help to provide you with the strength to cope with what has happened.

> 'Remember and focus on all the beautiful memories about the person'

As time goes by, you will gradually feel the pain a little less and you understand a bit better everything that's happened. You will slowly accept what you cannot change and can allow yourself to remember and focus on all the beautiful memories about the person. Sometimes the pain never fades entirely, but remembering the beauty brings you a certain level of peace.

This is the type of feeling you can keep in your heart forever. You can remember the fun times, the friendship, the closeness, the beauty – and be grateful for the time you had with the person. You can be thankful for having had the opportunity of knowing him or her, and for what he or she brought into your life. You are free to treasure this person forever and can pray for his or her happiness.

58 When eating or exercise is a disorder

'I'm worried about a girl in my class. Kim has always been a cheerful, outgoing girl, but during the last few months something has changed. She's looking pale, thin, is much quieter and either forgets to bring lunch to school or doesn't eat what she brings. She says her Mom feeds her too much at home, but her Mom once commented that Kim must be eating loads at school because she's never hungry at home. A few months back Kim's boyfriend broke up with her, saying that he was now going out with a girl who was much prettier than Kim. Could this have started the change in her eating habits?'

We all need to eat to stay alive, that's obvious. We also all have different relationships with the food we eat. Some of us love it for the taste and sensation we experience, some of us eat just because we have to and some of us develop a very different approach to what we eat.

Likewise, exercising is very important for our physical, mental and emotional wellbeing, but sometimes some of us start to see it in another light. Exercise is priceless when it comes to keeping us fit, looking well toned and glowing with good health, but it needs to be kept in balance for us to reap the benefits.

A range of relevant aspects is covered in Chapters 31 and 32, Your Body, and Exercise and you may find it useful to read those chapters before you continue with this one. The way you see yourself and the way you think others see you often affects your attitude to food and to exercise. Because how and what you eat influences the way you look, you may be tempted to give food more power than it deserves. There are those, too, who might give too much power to exercise.

Some meanings food can have

☀ **Life-source.** Your body can stay alive only if you feed it, so you have no alternative, you have to eat.

☀ **A treat**. Delicious food can add a dimension of enjoyment into your life. For some people food represents far more than nutrition. From the creative expression of producing delectable dishes, to the taste-bud tantalising experience of savouring a favourite meal, those individuals enhance their life through food.

☀ **A comfort or an escape**. For some of us, food can be a comfort during emotionally difficult times. It gives us 'something to do', it provides our body with extra strength, it's something familiar and it can feel comforting.

☀ **Protection**. For some people, their way of coping with hurt and emotional pain or insecurity is to build a protective cover around themselves. Food is a way of physically achieving this. By increasing their weight they may subconsciously feel that they are increasing their insulation against the pain.

☀ **Punishment**. If, for some reason, some people feel they deserve to be 'punished', food can become one of the tools they select. They may eat too much or too little. They may even fluctuate between the two by over-eating, feeling guilty and then getting rid of what they've eaten.

☀ **A solution to a hidden pain**. Sometimes something can happen which causes you deep emotional pain. Perhaps you were overweight as a child and were teased about it. Perhaps you had a traumatic childhood and you feel hurt, ashamed or embarrassed by it. Perhaps you were (or are) in an abusive relationship, either physically or emotionally.

Whatever the reasons, and there could be hundreds of different ones, people sometimes see eating habits as the solution to their pain. If you feel that in some way you are not good enough, you might start to focus obsessively on your external appearance. It is easy to make yourself believe that if only you could look good then all your problems would go away. What you don't realise is that very often the way you think you look is influenced by the experiences you've had. For example, if you've repeatedly been put down by someone, then you can start to see yourself the way you think that person sees you.

If you decide that becoming thinner will solve your problem you may become so obsessed by this aim that you fail to see yourself in a true light. It is then so easy to get caught up in the mistaken belief that you have to eat less and less. Whenever you look at yourself all you will start to see is imperfection. What you don't realise is that the 'imperfection' lies in your mind and your emotions and it cannot be fixed by manipulating what you eat.

Is food ever a problem or a solution for you?

If you ever feel that you are starting to see food as a cause of or a solution to the problems in your life, then you need to take a really good look at the overall state of your life. Identify all the reasons that are making you believe that addressing your food intake will solve your problems. Then identify someone you could talk to about this.

When depriving your body of the food it needs becomes a solution, that's when you need to check this out with someone who is qualified to work out the best and real solution for you. You may not even realise or acknowledge that food is taking on more significance than it should, so check it out if you just have a vague suspicion. In most cases, a need to withhold or purge food has nothing to do with weight at all. It usually has to do with some other complex issues which you need to identify and resolve.

If you're not sure whether your eating habits could become unhealthy, ask yourself these questions:

* Do you feel life would be easier or happier if you could lose weight or if you changed your eating habits?
* Do you feel you are not 'good enough' in terms of others' (or your own) expectations?
* Are you aware of trying to eat as little as possible?
* Do you ever want to make yourself throw up after a meal?
* Do you take laxatives as an attempt to keep your weight down?
* Has anyone ever told you that you are too thin? What was your reaction?

If you answered 'yes' to any one of these questions then you need to speak about what you're thinking and feeling to someone who can help you. You could well be heading for trouble if you're not in some already.

Exercise addiction — could you be a candidate?

Excess of any kind is often detrimental in the long term so, on a regular basis, it's good to check whether what you're spending a great deal of time on is as positive for you as it should be.

Nowadays we all know about the benefits of exercise, but over-exercising is becoming increasingly common, and this can lead to exercise addiction. You can become addicted to exercise for one of these reasons:

You may get hooked on the high caused by the 'happy chemicals' (endorphins) your body produces when you work out.

You may see exercise as a way to losing weight and getting thinner and thinner, and you start to obsess about the effects.

You may use exercise as an escape from some troubling reality.

You may be striving to excel as a sportswoman in fields that demand a specific weight, body type or looks, such as: runners, gymnasts, ice skaters or dancers.

Exercise is one of the best methods for weight control, but maintaining the right balance is important. Exercise addiction among teenagers is frequently linked to a desire for weight-control and has elements in common with anorexia and bulimia. Instead of starving or purging, they work off all they have eaten – and more – through exercise.

If you're unsure about whether you could be running into dangerous territory, ask yourself some questions:

☀ Are you exercising (running or working out at a gym) for more than an hour a day, seven days a week?
☀ Do you exercise even if you have serious physical injuries?
☀ Do you skip school or work, or even social engagements in order to exercise?
☀ Do you harbour feelings of low self-esteem, depression or anger?
☀ Are you obsessed with your weight and feel prepared to drive your body into the ground in your attempts to lose weight through exercise?

Your answers to these questions will give you an indication of whether you possibly are becoming addicted to exercise. If you suspect that you could be in addictive mode, then it's important to find someone who can help you out of it.

When should you ask for help?

Asking for help is a sign of strength, never weakness. Some more thoughts about this are covered in Chapter 53, When You Need Help and you might find it useful to glance at them now. I can't stress enough how important it is for you to be able to seek help, advice or support if you ever find that you're heading for a possible 'eating or exercise habits problem'. This is not something you'll easily solve on your own and the longer you leave the situation unresolved,

> 'Very often the way we think we look is influenced by the experiences we've had'

the harder it will become to sort out. Don't risk damaging your body. Don't jeopardise your future happiness. Ask for help and make the effort to give yourself the attention and assistance you deserve. You're worth it.

59 if tragedy strikes

'A couple of weeks ago my closest friend, my beloved soulmate, was taken away from me. One minute he was driving to work, the next minute a large petrol-tanker skipped a red light – and he was gone. We'd met at the age of ten and we've been inseparable ever since. He knew my every thought, dream and fear, and I knew his. He supported me through my childhood health problems, my academic achievements, the death of my dog, and the traumatic death of my Mum. Now he too is gone. It's as if someone has ripped out a vital part of my being. A light has gone out somewhere and the world around me looks like a dimly lit tunnel. How, oh how do I cope with something like this?'

Sometimes, something happens which is much worse than any of the ups and downs you've ever faced before, and tragedy enters your life. Perhaps it's someone's death. Maybe it's a divorce or a terrible accident. It usually has to do with the loss of something very dear to you.

When it happens, it feels as if your whole world has caved in. It can be so traumatic that you feel as though you cannot possibly survive this. You feel that life will never be the same again and that you may never know happiness again.

I am dealing with this subject to share with you some of the feelings that might well up at this time and to tell you that you're not alone. When tragedy strikes, we often do feel so alone. It feels as if no-one else could possibly understand what we're going through. It can even be surprising that life goes on as usual for others. The sun still shines, babies are born and people fall in love. For a time we seem to be excluded from that world.

If this ever happens to you, then my heart reaches out to you because those of us who've been there know the agony of facing tragic reality. We know about gut-wrenching sadness, about crying until your heart feels as if it might burst, about the suffocating hopelessness, desperate loneliness and the fear of not coping.

People may try to help as best they can. Sometimes they do wonders and other times their efforts may be misguided. Don't resent their attempts. They care about you and they're doing their best. They may try to explain that everything happens for the best, that God will help or that time is the best healer, but when you're in the depths of your pain none of these well-meant thoughts do much good.

When tragedy strikes it brings unavoidable pain. Tragedy is like an unexpected waterfall in the river of your life. It suddenly sweeps you away, battering you as you fall. When you arrive at the bottom you need to get away from the turbulent part, you need to acknowledge your pain and then you need to let the river sweep you away. For a while you need to float along, until you've emptied all your initial grief. Grab a log for support if you can find one and let yourself be swept along.

Finding a landing place

You might encounter rapids and waves, but eventually the waters will grow shallow and calm. Then, slowly, raise your head and take a look around. See where you are, notice that the sun does still shine and take in the passing scenery. Compose your thoughts and start to keep a lookout for a good landing place. It might be an island which will do temporarily, or it may be a permanent harbour. It may be tempting to let yourself sink beneath the waves, but giving up isn't the answer. You were born with an inner strength and you now need to find it.

The log and the landing place I am referring to is someone or something that will help you cope. The log could be the closest available person and the landing place could be a more definite and long-lasting help. Letting yourself initially go with the flow is allowing yourself to feel the pain. If you try to resist and suppress your anguish, it'll just hide and wait to emerge sometime later. Suppressing it can make things much worse in the long run. It can even end up making you ill.

When you've experienced tragedy you'll be fragile for quite some time and it's important to try to find someone who will be able to give you the help you need. You need the most help you can get – so don't be afraid to ask for it. By avoiding help and by trying to cope on your own you make the healing process much more difficult.

As time goes by, your wounds will slowly start to heal. Some pain may remain in your heart, but the intensity will gradually ease. Always try to think about what you can do to make things easier for yourself. Spend time with your friends and get involved in activities you'll enjoy. Keeping yourself busy and focusing on the good things in your life can see you through the hardest part.

'Tragedy is like an unexpected waterfall in the river of your life'

For real healing to take place you need to start looking to the future and doing things that will bring you pleasure, comfort and joy. Later, much later, you might look back and see how you've grown through everything that happened. By surviving and by coming through the pain, you acquire a new type of strength and wisdom. This wisdom will in turn bring you renewed strength and may even help you if one day you're needed to help someone else.

60 where danger lurks

'My Mum is a born worrier and she just can't understand that I'm now 16, no longer a child, and that I can look after myself perfectly well. She's forever asking me about where I'm going, who I'll be with, who's driving, whose house I'll be spending the night at, and whether there may be any drugs or alcohol. I know that she trusts me, but I do wish she'd realise that the world is actually quite a safe place...'

Much as we don't like to dwell on dark and unpleasant things, they do unfortunately exist and knowledge is better than ignorance. I have included this chapter as a result of specific requests by mothers who are concerned for their daughters' safety. It covers a very relevant issue and lists those situations that can easily arise and that, if you're unprepared, can be traumatic or dangerous. I'm not trying to make you panic, I'm just trying to raise your awareness.

Hitchhiking

Don't ever hitch a lift. There are too many people with unpleasant intentions and it's not worth risking your wellbeing or even your life for the sake of transport. You might have friends who frequently hitchhike and they'll no doubt tell you that there's nothing dangerous about it. You only have to read the papers, in most parts of the world, to find out about all the things that do go wrong. Even countries which up until recently were considered very safe (much of Europe can be included here) now have many tragic hitchhiking tales to tell.

Stranger danger

Be wary of strangers. It's sad to have to say, but befriending a stranger can be extremely risky. It depends to a certain extent on where you are and you have to be able to judge this for yourself in some situations. At your age you are at the biggest risk of ill-intentioned strangers and this is a fact. If someone you don't know suddenly approaches you and starts a conversation, your first reaction should be wariness. Until you know the reason for approaching you and you're convinced that all is above board, your wariness should remain. Sinister reasons span a wide range of possibilities and can include a sexual advance, drugs, kidnapping or merely drawing you into unsuitable company. There's usually something for the stranger to gain and for you to lose.

Clubs and 'open' parties

Not everyone goes to clubs and parties to have a good time. Among the partygoers will be those who are scouting for easy targets for their own purpose (most often sexual or theft-related). The most common incident is the 'spiking' of someone's drink with some kind of drug. Unless you are familiar with and trust all those present, *never* leave your drink unattended. If you leave it while you're dancing, get a fresh one later. Some people even advise buying canned drinks only, due to the ease with which drinks in a bottle or a glass can be tampered with.

Don't accept anything to smoke and make sure you have a reliable lift home. If you're uncomfortable with any of the goings-on at the event, don't hesitate to leave. If you're relying on a lift, phone someone to come and fetch you. Don't ever feel embarrassed about leaving an uncomfortable situation. If you don't look after yourself, who else will?

Danger from the most unlikely sources

Not everyone you know may have the same values as you do. This can be a hard reality to accept, but it's true. It would be wonderful if you could trust everyone you know, but unfortunately you can occasionally encounter 'troubled' people. I'm referring here to friends' relatives, friends' friends, domestic staff, your own date and even, sometimes, your own relatives.

If you ever receive any kind of approach which makes you uncomfortable, raise an immediate objection. Report the incident to someone you can trust and don't let yourself be threatened into keeping quiet about what happened.

The most common incidents are sexual, but they can be linked to drugs, finances or otherwise. If anything like this happens, you'll no doubt feel very shaken and you may wonder whether you perhaps did something to encourage the approach. In virtually all cases you are completely blameless. You are just the innocent victim of a sick individual.

The same applies to that sickening experience called 'date rape'. When you're out on a date with someone you don't know well, it's important to retain a fair amount of caution

> 'Knowledge is better than ignorance'

and vigilance. Even if you're with someone who was introduced to you by a friend, but more so with someone you may have met outside of your normal circle of friends, be alert and avoid being completely alone with him. Date-rape drugs are now so easy to obtain and guys with twisted values seem to be on the increase.

Even without drugs (and even if you know the guy well), if you find yourself alone or you engage in a heavy kissing and petting session, you're exposing yourself to the risk that the situation could get out of hand and you could end up in trouble or in danger. It's always good to be aware, not to let your guard down completely and also to have a plan of what you'll do in case things start to go wrong.

Driving

Whenever you are a passenger you owe it to yourself to be happy with the driver's abilities behind the wheel. If you feel at all unsafe, don't feel shy to ask the driver to drive more carefully. If you realise that he or she has had too much to drink, make an alternate plan for getting to your destination without engaging in any further debate. Such situations can feel very awkward when they arise and it takes guts to speak out. Those 'guts' could, however, save your life.

Staying over at a friend's house

'Sleepovers' are usually great fun – and yet they're the source of much debate among parents. If we know the parents of your friend well and we're happy with their values, then all is fine. Our worries come from the fact that this is a time when something can go wrong if the family you're staying with doesn't share your value system. There may be no supervision, someone may introduce behaviour you're uncomfortable with, a family member may make an unwelcome approach and then what? It happens more often than you realise. My suggestion is that if you're not certain about who's going to be there and what the family values are, then don't stay to sleep. If you ever find yourself in an unwelcome or disturbing situation, no matter what time it is, phone home immediately and ask to be fetched.

Going out at night

When you're going out, either on a date or to meet friends somewhere, it's important that you go about it in the right way. Let your parents know the details of where you'll be and with whom, and agree on the time you'll return, means of transport and any other arrangements. Don't see your discussion as a lack of independence or an invasion of privacy – see it as a routine safety measure.

Always have a friend with you, because going out alone at night is never a good idea. You never know what situation you might encounter. If you have a boyfriend let your parents meet him, and listen if they express an opinion about him (they inevitably have your interests at heart, so even if you disagree with their comments don't discount them until you can prove them wrong).

It's also essential to make sure that someone you trust will be available to come and fetch you in case you run into difficulties. Keeping the communication channels with your parents flowing makes the whole process of swopping information about plans and arrangements smooth and hassle-free. Rebelling creates unnecessary tension and friction, and can lead to bad decisions that could place you in jeopardy.

Toilets, travel and being alone

You're always more vulnerable when you're on your own. It's a fact. Whether you're travelling the world or going to the toilet in a shopping centre, be aware of your surroundings, especially if you're on your own. Single people are easier to prey on and there's much to be said for the philosophy of 'safety in numbers'. If you're travelling, never leave your luggage unattended, even for a few seconds. If you need to elicit a stranger's help, avoid finding yourself in an isolated place. Keep to public places and don't accept invitations to a stranger's home. You obviously need to use your judgement here and take decisions that feel right after you've considered all your options. If you're accompanying the owner of your B&B it's somewhat different to accompanying someone you've just met at the station.

I don't want to fill you with paranoia. I just want to highlight the kinds of things that can (and do) happen and to raise your awareness of possible dangers. Be aware, keep your wits about you and stay safe!

Thank you, to my daughter Dominique

Thank you. Thank you for being in my life. Thank you for teaching me all the things I've learned from you and the things I've learned about because of you. I cherish the day you were born. It is a day that changed my life forever. It was the beginning of an experience I truly understood only once it happened to me – first the overwhelming awe at the miracle that had taken place and then the all-encompassing love that flooded my whole being. I never knew it was possible to feel such intensity of love and emotion. You are the greatest gift that was ever granted to me. Thank you for being my inspiration in writing this book. I love you.

An invitation

How do you feel about this book? I invite you to share with me any thoughts or questions you may have after reading it. If you have other topics you would like covered, or if you have specific thoughts to be considered for a following book, I would gladly hear about them.

Write to info@lifetalk.co.za or visit www.lifetalk.co.za

Acknowledgements

Life Talk is a mix of the various lessons and experiences that life has brought my way. Along my journey, so many people crossed my path and influenced forever the direction and learning that my life would take. I cherish their presence in my life.

Deep gratitude and a very special place in my heart is reserved for my mother. I see you still, I feel you near me, even though you're somewhere else now. I thank you for your love, for sharing your values with me, and for your unwaveringly positive approach to life. I treasure your wisdom, your patience, your courage, your laughter, your faith in God, your love of animals and nature and your undaunted spirit. I see you still, I always will, in my life's richness and in who I can be.

I thank my father who, in the short time we had together, conveyed his unswayable belief in integrity and ethics. That belief, together with his mischievous mind, his intellect and his literary and theatrical talent, provides me with a source of ongoing inspiration.

I thank the bosses and business partners I've had, for believing in me and for giving me my biggest career breaks. I thank our SilverLine team for the wonderful years we had in business, and for the growth we all encountered together. The lessons I learned during those years are now reflected in many of the practical guidelines in this book.

To my cousin Betula Jasienska, thank you for reading my early letters to Dominique and for enthusiastically urging me to turn what I was writing into a book. To Colin, thank you for being a good father to Dominique, and for initiating one of my life's steep growth curves.

I express my gratitude to my husband David Gates for re-entering my life at a very tough time, for holding my hand through the turbulence, and for giving me the enthusiastic encouragement I needed to get this book published. And I thank Harry, Bubbles, Les, Keith and Ian for welcoming me so warmly into the family.

Acknowledgements

I will always be grateful to all my friends for their enthusiasm and encouragement while I was writing *Life Talk*. I especially thank Annette Thompson for spurring me on in my writing, and for her and Nicolette Lowe's enthusiastic approach to everything I undertake.

Many thanks also go to the team at Struik/Oshun (South Africa) for publishing *Life Talk* so enthusiastically, to Laura Longrigg for her effort and help, to Nikki Read and the publishing team at How To Books, and to Melanie Jarman for her guidance during the UK editing process.

I thank God for bringing Dominique into my life, for providing me with the fortunate breaks I've received and for letting me learn my lessons (even the painful ones). Thank you too for inspiring me during the course of my writing.

I also express my gratitude to all my other friends, relations and colleagues who have touched my life and who have been a source of learning, inspiration and growth. Without the learning there would be no *Life Talk*.

(Reference was made in Chapter 48 to: *Who Moved My Cheese* by Dr Spencer Johnson.)